The View from
Babylon

ALSO BY DONALD RAWLEY

POETRY
Mecca
Malibu Stories
Steaming
Duende
Sirens

SPOKEN WORD
Odalisque

SHORT STORIES
Slow Dance on the Fault Line

NOVELS
The Night Bird Cantata

The View from Babylon

The Notes of a Hollywood Voyeur

Donald Rawley

WARNER BOOKS

A Time Warner Company

"The View from Babylon" originally appeared in *German GEO Magazine,* December 1994, as *"Von allen Engeln verlassen."*

"Hollywood" was originally commissioned by *German GEO Magazine.*

"Lunch at Harry Winston" originally appeared in *Buzz Magazine,* September 1996.

"Little Ghosts" originally appeared in *Buzz Magazine,* March 1994.

"Suicide in Las Vegas" originally appeared in *Buzz Magazine,* November 1994.

"Our Lady of the Lions" was originally commissioned by *Buzz Magazine,* July 1994.

"Nights with Tennessee" originally appeared in *Buzz Magazine,* August 1995, as "The Night Tennessee Williams Told Me He Loved Me."

Warner Books, Inc., 1271 Avenue of the Americas, New York, NY 10020
Visit our Web site at www.warnerbooks.com
Ⓦ A Time Warner Company

Printed in the United States of America
First Printing: July 1999
10 9 8 7 6 5 4 3 2 1

Library of Congress Cataloging-in-Publication Data

Rawley, Donald
    The view from Babylon : the notes of a Hollywood voyeur / Donald Rawley.
        p. cm.
    ISBN 0-446-52411-5
    1. Motion picture industry—California—Los Angeles—Miscellanea.
    2. Los Angeles (Calif.)—Social life and customs.   I. Title.
PN1993.5.U65R28   1999
384'.8'0979494—dc21
                                                                98-40034
                                                                CIP

Book design by Giorgetta Bell McRee

Contents

INTRODUCTION

My first encounter with the work of Donald Rawley came via my friend Beverly Bernstein, who in 1993 was editing a small L.A.–based literary magazine called *Mindscapes*. At that time I was penning flowery rejection notices under the name "Rita Roberts" (and to all who placed their trust in Rita, I am sorry). The phone rang in the afternoon. "Oh my God," Beverly said rapidly, in one long exhale, "I've just read the most amazing story and you're going to love it but we can't print it because it's got some upsetting stuff in it and it's kind of dirty."

My interest was piqued immediately. *Mindscapes* received many different kinds of manuscripts—mostly, I think, due to physical proximity—from the wan literary butterflies of UCLA Extension. There were tight-lipped, minimalist short stories about anorectic twentysomething women and their struggles to be understood by difficult sculptor men, men who perplexingly seemed to have no interest in them at all; weird 25-page-long science fiction rants about bombs and famines and the writer's rage about the precipitous plunge in "realistic plot lines" in the new *Star Trek*; the requisite amount of haikus about spring by the type of dreamy older citizen we associate with the name "Mildred."

But an excellent filthy story? Never.

The piece was Donald's short story "Shalimar." Rita Roberts loved it, as did Beverly and the rest of the staff (which at that time I think consisted of a husband and a dog), so, to the shock of our semi-vast readership, we published it. It was Donald's first published short story, which amazes me to this day. But *Mindscapes* soon made up for lost time: We continued to publish Donald in almost every issue.

All told, there were stories, poems (even though Ms. Roberts had told everyone we didn't publish poems—which was true, except that we did publish Donald's, because his were the only poems we ever actually liked), and even a truly memorable essay called "Is It Literary or Is It Commercial?" It was about the state of modern literature. Not surprisingly, Donald bemoaned it. What he found particularly execrable was the kind of timid, memoir-ish short story that began: "In the summer when I was twelve, in my grandmother's house in Vermont, I remember finding my sister Susan's box of private things . . ." Horrors, indeed!

Mindscapes eventually went the way of so many other magazines of the decade, but Donald Rawley's mini-revolution of the page continued to roar. In an era where the literary zeitgeist was a deadly earnest (bitterly multicultural, quietly incested, etcetera) woman in sensible Joan and David shoes, Donald's subject remained stinky, crass, tinselly old L.A., yon siliconed Sunset Plaza whore exploding out of a rubber bustier. But the sheer ferocity of Donald's vision paid off. Indeed, less than five years since the humble beginnings of "Shalimar," the mountain would finally come to

Mohammed—and by "mountain" I do mean *The New Yorker* (not to mention *Harper's*, *Story*, the Pushcart Prize, and major publishing houses in New York and England). It's with pride, joy and a kind of sloppy, cawing, *Cosmopolitan*-spilling delight that I cite these prestigious literary institutions in relation to Donald because, I'm telling you, this man really earned his East Coast imprimateur the hard way: in furs (if $100 beaver ones), in huge, garish, Trump-asonic jewels (if somewhat less than real, if bought on consignment of Ventura Boulevard in Sherman Oaks) . . . do you hear what I'm saying? This guy was alone in the Nineties! Fabulously alone. Donald would drive himself in his Cadillac (if elderly, if with a muffler problem) to a reading at A Different Light bookstore in Silverlake and all the other gay men would STARE.

However—military jackets encrusted with an unnervingly breezy mélange of fake combat medals aside (antoher of his signature "looks")—of all the identities, masculine and feminine, he tried on, Donald was first and foremost a writer. Donald is the only writer I've ever known who never complained about writer's block. Never. Donald's process never stopped, not even for a day. He wrote journalism for magazines, he wrote poetry for himself, he wrote when he was well, he wrote when he was sick. Toward the end of his life, in fact, he seemed frantic to finish everything. He felt time was short, and he wanted to leave a legacy. Happily, with more than half a dozen books of poetry, two novels, several anthologies of genre-busting short stories and even this, a collection of nonfiction essays, he more than has.

Barring a nuclear holocaust, or an overeager pulping station chez Barnes and Noble, our work will outlive us all. It's inevitable that stacks of our books will stand tall (and hopefully not all remaindered) long after our physical selves are gone. And so I focus my energy, for today, not on Donald's relatively early passing but on celebrating the guilty pleasure you're holding in your hands right now, *The View from Babylon*. A book about Los Angeles. Los Angeles: a literary construction, in Donald's own estimation, which is so very, very far from Vermont, your grandmother's house and Susan's box of secret things. (Unless, of course, Susan's box includes some cracked vials of cocaine, handcuffs, steroids of dubious extraction, and oddly sticky feather boa, some really big jewels and photographic evidence that Susan was once a man named Walter who ran a tanning salon in Mission Viejo.)

The View from Babylon is a great, wild and scary read, nothing socially redeeming about it. And I mean *nothing*. Frankly, there are sections that bring out even the Vermont on me. ("Vermont": a land to which I've never been. As Oscar Wilde might say if he were alive today, there is no such place as Vermont, and there are no Japanese.) There are passages in this book that, when I reread them, I put my head in my hands and say "Oh Donald. No. Don't go there. Not there. No. Donald. Look. You can't say—ho! No! No!" But he does. As usual, Donald breezes on, to a horizon only he can see (I picture this as a white line of sand beyond a tattered Miami beach, "Miami" being yet another literary construction), dragging us not just through Hollywood but the high desert, low desert, Las Vegas, Sherman

Oaks, Orange County—anywhere, really, that damaged people congregate. Although I should qualify that by noting that pretty much everyone stroked by Donald's elegant gold-nibbed pen emerges not just damaged but *fabulously* damaged.

In short, by the end of the book, you may not be sure what you think, but you certainly won't forget where you've been. And that, as some of us say, is literature. Or at least another masterful episode in an amazing literary oeuvre (pronounced "*OOOOOOOVRAH!*"— loudly, of course).

Sandra Tsing Loh
January 1999

The View from

Babylon

"And we're going to party like it's 1999."
—Prince

THE VIEW FROM BABYLON

Let us speak, briefly, of madness. On this August morning in Los Angeles there was a 3.6 aftershock at approximately 5:46 A.M. Enough to jolt me from sleep, it knocked over a small vase of flowers taken from the hospital in Sherman Oaks where my friend recuperates from viral pneumonia. Not to worry; no one here pays attention to tremors until they hit the big numbers: 4.5, 5.0. As for the pneumonia, I was told over the phone the night before that "that's what hospitals are for; they're good at that death thing."

Today it will be the hottest day in Los Angeles in the last one hundred years. Hell is being delivered to us in small increments. Over the past four years L.A. has become a confusion, a new vision of Apocalypse. Yet we still try to plot our lives by a swimming pool, talk to the right people, make correct decisions. We attempt beauty. Sometimes, in the madness, we succeed.

During the Northridge quake, my dining room collapsed, outside cement walls crumbled and windows blew apart in the early morning black. The hot January air was unusually dry, and shrouded in a stink of lemon blossoms. I grabbed a leftover red Christmas candle, lit it, and ran outside to see if my neighbors were alive. They were parked in their cars, motors running, lights and radios on. Looking up at the hills, I saw other head-lights, like fireflies, dotting the shadows.

I remember candle wax had covered my arm to the elbow, and I only noticed it at dawn. I had not felt any-thing.

Three blocks away, an apartment building cracked in half, from the center; its two elevators were forced up through the roof like beans out of a can. I remember walking through the rubble of my house and thinking, This has to be cleaned up. I'm having a dinner party in three weeks. Later I would go into shock for several hours. In three weeks I had my dinner party. A 5.2 hit several minutes before we sat down to eat, and no one said a word. Because this is how life works in Los An-geles.

People who survive here really have to be adrenaline junkies."

This statement is made by Samantha Dunn, a freelance journalist who teaches poetry to teenagers in South Central Los Angeles. We are driving in her new Nissan Sentra on the Ventura Freeway toward Malibu. We both know in her car we can have the air-conditioning on, speak privately, and just disappear for an hour.

Samantha is a beautiful, pale-skinned young woman with thick red hair. Her eyes stare straight ahead, into the freeway grit, as she explains why her Nissan is new. During the quake her neighbor's chimney fell on her car, flattening it to the ground.

"When I saw it hit, my husband and I started laugh-ing. Only in Los Angeles is your car going to be smashed by a metric ton of brick and you still want to go inside and fix yourself a cool drink. With ice."

"Are you an adrenaline junkie? Is that how you survive?" I ask this as a black couple in a Cadillac Eldorado in the lane next to us argue quite loudly. They see I am looking at them and they speed up, rolling up their windows as they pass. They continue arguing.

"The tension here is like a low-grade hum all the time, like static on the radio," Samantha murmurs. "When I go back to New Mexico for family visits, I feel as though I'm on another planet. It takes me days just to calm down from L.A."

The traffic begins to slow, due to an accident ahead. It is nearing sunset; soon the freeway will assume a new canvas, glittering and soulless. I switch the radio on. "Hypnotized," by Fleetwood Mac, is playing.

"I don't just survive here, I thrive," Samantha remarks quietly. "After the riots, it was a bit frightening going down to South Central to teach the kids, but I'm more frightened of being attacked, or my car stolen or house robbed, in my own neighborhood, than in South Central. With the rebuilding, it looks like Cairo down there. You don't know whether the buildings are going up or coming down."

"Or Beirut," I remark.

"I'm happy here. Los Angeles forces you to reassess who you are just about every day; this is the city where sometimes you might only have five minutes to grab what's left of your life and run. Everything that's happening here is going to happen to the rest of the world in ten years. We're the forefront."

"That's fine to say when you're young. In your twenties that kind of excitement works. But when you hit middle age, things change," I counter.

"Yeah, but right here and now, this is the most exciting city in the world. And the most dangerous, the most toxic."

Our car has stopped and the sun is setting in a crimson flush. Malibu is ten miles ahead; Topanga Canyon is to our left. We see a gasoline cargo truck on its side. There is an apparent gas leak on the highway. Two cars, a Ford and a Mercedes, are wrecked. There is an ambulance driving toward them. Much of the guardrail has been destroyed; traffic is being rerouted and police have set up emergency flares.

"What a beautiful sunset," Samantha says.

There is a firm belief here that the stranger at the door will be a killer simply by a lessening of odds. Rapists impersonate policemen, immigration officers, and doctors. Rapists sneak into backseats of unattended cars outside high schools and churches. Here rape is spiritual. Stay too long and you go home without a soul.

On Wednesday, August 10, 1994, a homeless couple living out of their station wagon, Kathyleen and Steven Giguere, were sentenced to six years in prison on felony child neglect charges in the death of their four-month-old son, Steven Jr. The infant was bitten over 110 times by a rat. Actual death occurred when the rodent's teeth struck an artery in Steven's wrist.

Steven Jr.'s corpse had air in its lungs, allowing a supposition he was screaming during the attack. Either Kathyleen was passed out from alcohol or drugs, or

Steven was alone in the station wagon, which was full of garbage and roaches. It was parked in an Anaheim parking lot, where the Gigueres begged, using their welfare money and spare change to buy methamphetamine and wine.

Disneyland was not far away. Perhaps the Gigueres panhandled in front of the theme park. Perhaps they forgot where the station wagon was, or the windows were rolled up for a reason only Kathyleen knows. Perhaps no one could be bothered to listen for a homeless baby crying as a rat chewed on its skin.

In the luridness we find our black mirror, the same mirror Truman Capote described Gauguin using at the turn of the century to relax his eyes after seeing too much color. With a black base, this instrument reduces all images to charcoals and grays, cooling the retina. Here in Southern California, at the turn of the century, we have seen too much color, and our eyes need to rest.

The studio of artist John Rose is located on Santa Fe Street in downtown Los Angeles. It is a Zenlike room, a long rectangle with bare, freshly painted white walls that seem electric when the northwestern light hits them. Six enormous cement columns divide the space, giving it the feel of an Egyptian temple. Art is stacked in corners.

From his windows John Rose can see two parking lots and the bridges over the Los Angeles River, with its midday dazzle of cement and oasis pockets of weeds and water. Beyond that he sees the rooftops of East L.A. I mention the view seems deserted.

"You're not looking close enough," Rose answers. "There are homeless camps under the bridge, drag queens luring in truck drivers at the far end of the parking lot, see? There's someone coming out from the bushes in the river with a fishing pole. The water's polluted, sewage, but he's fishing anyway. Now most of the queens are HIV positive. And most of those truckers they're blowing have a wife and kids. You figure it out."

My eyes become accustomed to the glare. Suddenly I see Rose is right. I see people in the fluid heat.

"It's like Babylon out there," Rose continues. "I've heard so many new languages I have no idea of, dialects, people I can't figure out what color, race, country. Even the homeless, particularly the mentally ill, have a new way of speaking to each other. New signals."

I notice a man about forty yards from John Rose's window sniffing from a bottle.

"The bottle is filled with gasoline," Rose notes. "This man fills it up every morning and sniffs it all day. I have never seen him so much as eat a sandwich. At dusk he begins to dance, like a dervish, in a constant circle, until he passes out. He does the same thing tomorrow, you know? I find it horrifying. But beautiful too. Almost like some sort of a shaman."

John Rose is fifty-two. He was born in Los Angeles and has lived here his entire life. For the past twenty years he has driven to his studio from an elegant house in Silver Lake.

"I like juxtaposition," Rose says. "I also love Los Angeles. L.A. is no longer an American city. It is another world entirely, the Queen of the Pacific Rim, like Miami is to the Caribbean."

I mention fear, crime. Rose shakes his head.

"No one here ever bothers to look at the past. People think the Northridge quake was the first big one! L.A. has always been violent. Look at Charles Manson. Before him, the Black Dahlia murder. There's a negative charge here, maybe the way the earth keeps shifting. It also brings creativity and excitement. My art doesn't change when an earthquake hits. I might change, but my art doesn't. That's what keeps me alive."

Overhead there is the sound of a helicopter's rotors, as though they are right above Rose's studio.

"They are," he answers. "My studio is in the direct line of police headquarters' helicopter launch pad. They fly over me day and night."

We watch two helicopters fly over us toward the Los Angeles River. They circle it for ten minutes, and people scatter; then they head toward Boyle Heights and East L.A.

"I know what you're thinking: Maybe I should find a quieter studio. I love it right here. Look at the light. The view. I'll never move."

Among the elite in Los Angeles you can never be too clean, smart, together, or rich. You must be all of the above, and more, in order to survive. If your Rolls is stolen outside a restaurant on La Cienega you immediately buy a Jeep Wagoneer; if you start to show lines in your face you begin aromatherapy, hydromassage. You elevate your mood with Prozac, or a Desyrel. If you need more sleep you take desipramine.

You make certain choices. You don't drink, because everybody in show business is in Alcoholics Anonymous. You don't smoke, because no public place will let you in Los Angeles. You admit to taking Prozac, but not to the fact that you have a vial of cocaine in your purse. If you have an affair, you are smart enough to conduct it in Honolulu or Mexico. If you get a divorce, you already have a fantastic prenuptial agreement.

You know how to play the game, and you are always covered. The game is still on in Los Angeles. In this world poverty and racism are meaningless, but the fluctuation in real estate values is not.

I am having lunch poolside with Roger Dauer, a real estate investor with a 13,000-square-foot home in Beverly Hills. The estate has nine bedrooms and thirteen baths, a three-thousand-square-foot living room, three carved oak bars, a ballroom with a baby grand piano, and a mural of Hollywood in blacklight paint. Upstairs there is a screening room that seats fifty, with mauve leather chairs and stereophonic sound.

"We're all poor in the nineties," Roger says, putting down his fork. "I lost a lot of money on Beverly Hills real estate. So did everyone else. The big moment, when the bubble burst, was around June of 1990. I realized my wife and I would have to make lifestyle changes. Less bullshit, more realism. Then the quake. I'm tired of L.A., but where do you go after Beverly Hills? Think about it. Everything is a step down."

"You've always been very comfortable, Roger," I say.

"Gail and I have two beautiful daughters just about

grown. Do you know anyone who wants an enormous mansion?"

"People are transferring huge assets from the Orient," I offer.

"There's been a lot of interest in this house from Hong Kong. And Macao," Roger notes, lowering his voice.

Somewhere below Sunset Boulevard I hear the faint sound of police sirens. The scent of Victorian rose-bushes drapes the air, and a fountain is trickling near the pool. Roger gets up for a Diet Coke and asks if I want one. I nod my head.

"Just one calorie," Roger says, winking.

I am still thinking of Steven Giguere Jr. in the back-seat of a station wagon in Anaheim, of helicopters beating over John Rose's studio. How I wake up each morning expecting a quake. Roger and I continue to chat about Pacific Rim investing and New Age music to de-stress by. Then we discuss security systems: when attack dogs and electrified fencing are absolutely nec-essary, how many of the major estates in Beverly Hills have 24-hour video surveillance, laser locks, whether or not household staff should carry loaded weapons.

When Roger asks me if I would like to see some new renovations in the house, I say yes, because that is, after all, a very constructive thing to do.

Beverly Hills–based psychologist Dr. Lewis Cozolino has written many articles on child abuse and schizo-phrenia; he sees Los Angeles as typifying modern angst.

"There are no seasons in L.A., hence no logic. People

are panicked about losing work, lifestyle. They work harder and make less money. The opportunity to relax is decreasing; people develop bad habits when they are under stress. Many get involved in meaningless activities. Others become obsessed with nutrition, body-building, excessive exercise."

"What about disasters?" I ask.

"Add fires destroying homes a mile away, earth-quakes, riots. There is a sense nothing may be here to-morrow. But there is more. L.A. is the essential narcissistic city. Because of the film business, genera-tions of very beautiful people have moved here, bred and settled. You have three generations of incredibly beautiful people living here. And in the business, peo-ple are not selected for their intelligence, depth or com-passion. It's all on looks."

I suddenly understand Cozolino. In an emotionally barren landscape, walls first have to be built before they can be electrified. You play by the rules or you don't play at all. No one in Los Angeles tells you what the rules exactly are. Because they shift, like the path of fire in a September wind. Life on the fault line tells us who will be considered beautiful, who will be cherished and who will not.

Yesterday there was a first-stage smog alert in the San Fernando Valley. Today it is canceled, as the Santa Ana winds have rolled through; but there is a fire in Santa Clarita, about a half hour from the city. Fire inspectors are worried. It is arson, because this fire was definitely set. It has already eaten away several hundred acres. No dwellings are threatened, yet. The fire marshal only says on the television, "We'll see where the wind takes it."

Ten aftershocks hit the West Valley this week. There are concerns for drought measures if rain doesn't come soon. My friend comes home today; outside the hospital the heat will reach one hundred degrees. No clouds.

I know I will be staying inside for the next three weeks, in air-conditioning. My front gate and door will stay permanently locked. My gardener sheared the brown fronds off my palm tree and found a nest of rats, dead from the heat. He will shear the other palms tomorrow.

I will begin to cut losses, reinvent myself. I will listen to Sadé and Tito Puente, the Mambo King. I will drink mineral water, begin vitamin injections. I will not accept social engagements until I look my very best. I will write on the expectations of hell, whether God exists, because I am still alive in Los Angeles. And I know many things.

HOLLYWOOD

A strong southern wind from Mexico is caressing the Hollywood Hills, whistling through a subtropical dusk. It is the kind of wind that dreams and sleep come from. I am in the penthouse of the Chateau Marmont hotel on Sunset Strip, and below me the lights of the Los Angeles basin are beginning to turn on.

This is the Howard Hughes suite, where the reclusive billionaire sat at a window with a pair of binoculars, studying the breasts of starlets sunning themselves at the hotel's pool. Many of the rooms here are named for their legendary inhabitants: a Garbo suite, a Frank Capra suite. There are no traces of Mr. Hughes left here, as the suite has been redone many times. Time is neither wasted nor standing still in Hollywood.

Nine floors below, two security guards, in matching beige police uniforms with gold accents, are guarding a billboard on Sunset Strip—an entire billboard of money: real five-, ten- and twenty-dollar bills under Plexiglas, covering the sign like wallpaper.

It is an advertisement for a luxury automobile. The make of the car doesn't matter. What does matter is *all* that money on Sunset Strip. The guards yawn, readjust their mirrored sunglasses. Tourists stop. Take pictures.

Above the hotel, nestled against a glamorous section

of the hills, night-blooming jasmine has begun releasing its scent, and it's drifting through the penthouse's open doors.

I am attending a private party for a major talent agency and the atmosphere tonight is—in an almost comical way—exactly what is expected of Hollywood. There are beautiful women in tight sequined cocktail dresses, men with photogenic noses. Conversation is hushed, important. Staff scurry with silver trays of soft-shell crab, sushi and Beluga caviar.

I will be here less than an hour. Parties in Hollywood are seldom private but organized to raise money for charities or to promote films. Once "in the business," a producer or director gets busy. There is little time for the elegance of entertaining at home, or for personal friendships.

Why be bothered with being a friend to someone who isn't going to help you? This distinct chasm between Hollywood and the rest of the world is born from both self-aggrandizement and necessity. If you work steadily, many months of the year are spent on location or on the lot; when a film is being made, nothing else matters.

People in the business tend to view their work, industry status and *connections* as more important than riots, earthquakes or floods. The only two things that will ever shut down the film business are lack of funds or a nuclear war.

When I recently telephoned a producer friend of mine, he informed me that he hadn't stepped inside his house on Mulholland Drive, at the top of the Hollywood Hills, since the January '94 quake. When I commented that his damage must have been extensive, he corrected me.

"Oh no," he blithely remarked. "The house and the dogs are fine. My wife is suing me for divorce, though. Our housekeeper takes care of everything."

He explained to me how he was on his way to Madrid, then Cannes, when the quake hit. He took care of distribution rights for several projects at Cannes, flew to Paris for meetings with Credit Lyonnaise, then flew to London for what he described as a "masturbation session with the Brits. Their film business has been in the toilet for thirty years and they still think they own the world. Jesus."

In London he realized he'd be wasting time returning to Los Angeles for "all that mess" and his wife's hysteria, so he flew to New York, rented an office and a hotel apartment, and produced two teenage comedies, both low budget, while waiting on studio money and talent signatures for a much larger project he'd acquired.

His wife is now suing him for exactly half, under California law, of everything they own. He has arranged a good settlement for her, under the condition she lays no claim to future film projects or the income resulting from those projects. Their divorce paper is over a hundred pages long. When I mentioned he'd ruined his personal life and lost half of everything he once owned, there was a silence, then a cheerful remark.

"Yeah, but I got solid backing now. I got great *connections.*"

The majority of divorces in Hollywood occur because someone is always away on location. And it is an unspoken rule that everyone, from technical to cameramen to even the stars, sleep around on location. Everyone knows this. Everyone.

Tonight I see three important directors, one major

producer and one female Oscar winner from a few years back, in tight black jeans, a tight black T-shirt, no makeup and no brassiere.

Several film deals will be put together. From a handshake, a whisper, a nod of the head. It seems simple in that the most important part of the game is getting the money. Leading up to that handshake, whisper and nod of the head at the penthouse at the Chateau Marmont have been months in negotiations with writers, agents and studio vice presidents. But only a few people finally make the decision, and those few socialize on the same circuit, and they have decided to socialize tonight.

The films resulting from tonight may be four or five years away, but the financing will be sought tomorrow morning. The female Oscar winner will smile, knowing she'll be working the summer of 1998. She'll drive home, fax her agent with the news and possibly double her going rate of $2 million per film.

This new doubling and tripling is not unusual. During the early Nineties, Jim Carrey and Sylvester Stallone doubled their salaries to $20 million per film, which rubs off on lesser, though still viable, names. Val Kilmer, since *Batman,* upped his ante to $10 million for his latest picture.

Executives scream bloody murder, but the truth is they have created this by turning film actors into commodities. Today Hollywood product makes a fortune in Europe, Africa, the Far East and South America. Consider all merchandising tie-ins, with Batman dolls, Stallone T-shirts, books, magazines, breakfast cereals—and actors and their agents will of course ask for top dollar, as a career doesn't last forever. The odds are that sooner or later you'll bomb. Big time.

The female Oscar winner in the tight black T-shirt knows, for example, that she went from a half-million dollars per picture—"the Gobi desert," a television actress once said to me—to a million dollars plus when she received her Oscar. She then decided to be "artistic" and make two serious, high-quality flicks, which urinated at the box office. Now she's playing the game again, and the big boys want her for a "big picture."

A "big picture" is this: action adventure, appealing to a male thirteen-to-thirty-year-old audience; a high-concept thriller, such as *Basic Instinct* or *Disclosure,* appealing to a wide demographic; or a romantic comedy with top talent and low overhead, like *Sleepless in Seattle.*

Your marketability depends not just on your box office or your awards, but if a fourteen-year-old boy will be standing in line to see you, and recognizes *your name*. And the men across the room here at the Chateau Marmont know this. And they are the big boys. And our Oscar-winning actress is smiling at them until her teeth hurt. Nineteen ninety-eight is not that far away, after all.

This is what is known as *Hollywood time.* It is not five days a week, nine to five, with holidays. It is breakfast and lunch, deal closings and preproduction. Film to film, and when you're working, everybody seems to get old but you. Then zero, and you're on your own.

The life that revolves around film reflects the nature of film itself. A movie is seldom shot in continuity (one scene following the other as dictated by the screenplay), and the resulting sensibilities of those involved in the making of movies are the same. In order to create one form of life on celluloid, another has to be sacrificed. The real world is another planet.

We are clever in Hollywood. We never speak to people who aren't "in the ring." We don't answer the phone or socialize with those outside "the business." We have our own language, intuitive and sexual. When we say "They're in bed together," it means two producers are working on a picture. For now, they're friends, sharing profits.

And profits are plentiful. Hollywood money never seems quite *real* to the rest of the world, partly due to the theory that we actually have to work to earn our keep. Joan Didion in *The White Album* very shrewdly pointed out how a major producer will explain why, two years after a film is released and is a hit, he receives a check for $11,400,000.00 for his share of final profits. No one really *needs* $11,400,000.00—but it is a check, a real tender, and the fact that it shows up on the producer's desk two full years after the fact is icing on an old, slightly stale cake. It is difficult to explain why anyone deserves $11,400,000.00 for taking six meetings at Morton's during the spring of 1993, but if questioned, the producer will gladly refer to his lawyer, who will explain the "whys" of this kind of money, in full, as the lawyer will have garnered at least ten to fifteen percent of that $11,400,000.00, because he drew up the contract. Only the numbers are bigger since Didion's tenure.

This is the New Hollywood. It will be the last great hustle of the new century approaching, one of the only ways left to make, or lose, big money. We are no longer living in the dream state we grew up in. The Hollywood our parents and grandparents knew no longer exists, except as nostalgia.

Stars get a picture made, one constant that hasn't changed. Hollywood's "true elite" consists of stars who can "open" a movie and two times out of three guarantee good box office. The list goes up and down, and the majority of the "true elite" are men.

On any given day, according to the vagaries of production schedules, the studios in Hollywood have less people working than is thought. Disney is the largest, with over 70,000 employees worldwide, but only 3,500 regulars on its palatial, cartoon-architecture lot in Burbank. MCA-Universal has approximately 9,000 employees on the lot; Paramount perhaps 2,500 to 8,000, including their television stages.

Movies are still a glamorous business. Those faces on screen are larger than life, and it is a closed, mysterious business, this making of stars and fortunes.

Playing the Hollywood game now requires very deep pockets; we are seeing an excitement here that is unparalleled. Companies are being bought or newly formed. And the deals are becoming beyond mortal imagination.

Recently Steven Spielberg, David Geffen and Jeffrey Katzenberg formed their own studio, Dreamworks SKG. Their "start-up" money: $2 billion. Each of the three partners has kicked in $33.3 million. Microsoft, the software company, has pledged an initial $27 million for a 1 percent profit share. Investor Paul Allen is in Dreamworks for $500 million. Chemical Bank is offering Dreamworks a *billion*-dollar line of credit. The three men are still looking for property on which to build their studio and are producing movies regardless.

I remember standing poolside at the Peninsula, waiting for the big boys to make their appearance. Four hundred television, video, still cameras. At least. From around the world. I was speaking to a writer from *Los Angeles Weekly* and a porno director, of all things. Lots of cocktails. Lots of laughs. And still not quite noon.

As we moved toward the already packed lobby, past the manicured grounds, a strong breeze blew up and I, as well as my two companions, were suddenly covered with tiny pink and white flowers.

"What is this, bougainvillea?" the *Weekly* writer asked, her hair blowing around her sunglasses.

"Palm blossoms," declared the porno director, with a sense of authority. "It's that time of year."

"You're both wrong. They're cherry blossoms. Smell them. We're covered in cherry blossoms," I said. We decided to not brush ourselves off in the lobby.

It was, quite simply, a Hollywood moment. Lots of them here. Too many, actually.

In a recent interview George Lucas, the creator of *Star Wars* and the Indiana Jones series, said about the new multimedia developments: "In a movie, you can lose thirty to sixty million dollars in the blink of an eye. In this new game, it's going to be billions in the blink of an eye. It's a very big game."

The Japanese have invested in Hollywood and lost their shirts. Sony and other corporations based in Tokyo regret the day they shook hands with the likes of Peter

Guber and Jon Peters, who ran Columbia Pictures. The Japanese, taking George Lucas's remarks into frame, have lost over two billion dollars and counting. Because the Hollywood they *thought* they were buying—the Hollywood of efficient studios, stars and glamour and steady profits—is gone, just as the Hollywood our parents sighed about is gone.

The Japanese did not realize it's a hustle here, not a plan or a set of rules. There are no rules in Hollywood, except to those we want to keep out. And that one rule is this: You aren't allowed in, unless you're prepared to put up the bank.

Tie-ins make Hollywood studios and deal makers astonishing sums. The box-office animated hit *Pocahontas,* from Disney, has a tie-in with the United States' number-two hamburger chain, Burger King (McDonald's is number one). Burger King pays a full fee for licensing the names and products, and Disney also gets a percentage of each item sold. Currently, during this tie-in period of up to six weeks or more from the opening of the film, Burger King has sold Pocahontas Kids Club Meals at the rate of 8 million per week, at approximately $2.00 a meal.

The toy maker Mattel, based in the suburb of Los Angeles called El Segundo, predicts a take-in of over $100 million from sales this year of Pocahontas dolls and related toys; the Pocahontas dolls will be made from existing Barbie molds.

This is how Hollywood infiltrates itself into popular culture. Your new Pocahontas doll has the same figure as Barbie, so you can dress them both up. You can eat a Pocahontas burger or wear a *Congo* T-shirt and baseball cap and feel like you're somehow part of it all. Because, unfortunately, you are.

I leave the party at the Chateau Marmont with Andrea, twenty-nine years old, who's married to the head of production at a major studio. Andrea wears subdued clothing, her jewels are simple, her blond hair is pulled back in a ponytail. We are on our way to Eclipse, a restaurant, in Andrea's chauffeur-driven Bentley.

At Eclipse, Andrea notes in a low voice that it is an "off night." A lot of agents and "television people." Except for two high-powered producers in a dark corner.

There is an unwritten but changing law on the Hollywood circuit. Monday nights are to be seen at Morton's; Tuesday, pizza at Spago. On Wednesday you go to Victor Drai's on La Cienega, if you can get a reservation. And on Friday night it's Eclipse, Muse or Citrus. No one goes out on Saturday or Sunday. That's for the public.

"Well, *they're* back in the ring," Andrea notes, smiling at the producers.

It takes a good five years—always figure five years—to get a movie made. It starts with the script. If it's a good script, and you're lucky enough to have a good agent, he'll pitch it to one of hundreds of vice presidents at the studios, ineffectual men in well-tailored suits whose job it is to say *no*. If he's a smart agent, he takes quite a few of these nephews and sons of the big boys to lunch and dinner, and finally one will say yes. Then the screenwriter and agent will go in and pitch the script. Forget art. The only important moment at a pitch meeting is who the stars can be, how much could the film make and what it is about, *in one sentence.*

Producers are not intellectuals and they are not interested in depth or "dramatic possibilities." Producers in Hollywood hate writers, feel that writers aren't necessary, and writers despise producers. This is a strange constant in Hollywood, possibly because film, in its essence, competes with the written word and ultimately negates it. In Hollywood, the writer must realize that film is a collaborative medium and that he sells his rights when he sells his script. The writer is considered the least important person on a set, and the most disliked. There is an old joke about an actress who wasn't too bright and so was sleeping with the writer. The picture becomes clear.

"Writers are a pain in the ass," notes a producer friend of mine, Michael. "They whine about money so we pay them well, then when the script undergoes changes they whine it isn't their original vision. Tough. They sold their vision to us, and now *we* do all the work."

It seems Michael, who is forty-three years old, with a dark beard shaved once a month, a baseball cap worn backwards on his head in the style of Mexican gangs, has not really grown up, and never will. Having optioned two of my scripts over the past four years and put me through countless (although paid) rewrites, which were then scrapped, along with my renewal, Michael is not one of my favorite people. Currently we are civil. An armed truce.

Michael is what is commonly known in Hollywood as a "screamer." Michael screams at his lawyers, and his secretaries, who generally last less than six weeks. Michael screams at his line producers, the technical crews, writers like myself and their agents. Never at the actors. Which is unfortunate, because sometimes they should be screamed at. Michael likes to scream so much he keeps a throat spray in the glove compartment of his Jaguar convertible. Which, of course, is leased.

There are other big-time screamers, although it is frowned upon. Producer Joel Silver is legendary for his tantrums. Lynda Obst, director Oliver Stone and executive Scott Rudin are to be avoided at all costs, if you value your life. There has always been an exhilaration and power at controlling vast amounts of people and money, and it is easy to abuse that power.

I hung up the phone the first time Michael screamed at me, thinking, I don't need this, no one in their right mind needs this, and the phone rang again, within seconds: Michael apologizing. It was then I realized I was dealing with a child, a greedy and unfocused but very shrewd child. In Hollywood, you don't *have* to behave.

An executive producer is responsible for getting the money; "producers"—just producers—are responsible for getting the film *made:* the daily shoots on budget, keeping the cast and crew working smoothly, everything in on time. Everyone has an assistant, not because of ego but because if someone should become ill the operative film unit must continue. The executive producer is paid a set fee, for his services, and a full fee, noted in legal contracts "from the first dollar made." Notice the word "profit" is not used. This is why certain producers get that check for $11,400,000.00 after the fact.

These are the men who say yes to projects. These are the men who still have their first dollar and have constructed their business dealings to never lose money. Creative accounting at the Hollywood studios is still the most watched, and least understood, part of the business. The active players in Paramount's mammoth hit *Forrest Gump*—star Tom Hanks, producers Wendy Finerman, Steve Tisch and Steve Sharkey, and director Robert Zemekis—all walked away with money up front and percentages "from the first dollar made." Assuming the film cost approximately $50 million to produce, including star salaries (and minus future residuals), it *looks* like Paramount made tons of money, which actually it did. A studio like Paramount will charge itself a distribution fee for the picture, which, in simple terms, the studio keeps. That's money in the bank. The cost of advertising—say $30 million for *Forrest Gump* (actually it was more, around $65 million)—is later used as a tax write-off, so *that's* money in the bank.

But when the writer of the novel *Forrest Gump*, Winston Groom, assumes that he is going to get a percentage of "net" profit, a Hollywood studio will tell him there is no "net" profit, only a gross that others in the film, like Tom Hanks and Steve Tisch, will be drawing their money from. Hanks will make close to $50 million or more on *Forrest Gump* because his contract is rock solid. No Hanks, no Gump, no $300 million.

Winston Groom became very public in his outrage, but he should have taken his cue from columnist Art Buchwald. There is no such thing as "net" profit in Hollywood. When I first came here, and even later, I always knew the only way you would ever make that enormous, unreal "Hollywood" money is to ask for a point of the gross.

But of course films often flop, leading to a chasm in the psyche. Hollywood, like Las Vegas, is a gambling town. Sexual and intellectual energy is lowered because the *real* attention, by both men and women, is "on the deal." In Las Vegas, when a gambler loses, it's *his* loss. In Hollywood, if a film doesn't fly, a lot of people lose *credibility*. This leads to a loss of power, and this will never change. It is a dictate engraved on more than one tombstone at Hollywood Memorial Cemetery.

Hollywood is also a town, fairly decrepit, with a Chinese Theatre and a Walk of Fame, and its very own sign, made of steel letters painted white.

Hollywood Hills. Sunset Boulevard. Hollywood Boulevard. By geographic definition, that's it. Hollywood is a way of thinking, and it is what I have always referred to as "the invisible city." Tourists are disappointed with Hollywood. They don't realize actual Hollywood is dismal. But they adore Beverly Hills and Sunset Strip, because this is what they believe "the invisible city" to be: someplace rich and glamorous and full of beautiful people. Sort of like what the Japanese corporations thought in the Eighties.

To get to the Hollywood sign, you drive first through the seedier neighborhoods of Franklin Avenue, once considered quite exclusive, then up through Beachwood Canyon to "Hollywoodland," a community of older Spanish and Italianate homes that have their own neighborhood grocery store and coffee shop.

Currently the sign is being renovated with much local fanfare. We know it is a symbol across the world. But we who live here know it is only amusing as a destination for sexual trysts and the occasional suicide.

No one in the current Hollywood power structure admits to actually *living* in Hollywood, although the hills are full of beautiful homes.

Hollywood is dangerous. Recently a psychotic stalker was shot by security guards inside Madonna's house; bullets entered his lower abdomen and one arm. He insisted over and over he was the singer's husband. He was armed, and kept saying how well he knew her, how much he loved her.

What he didn't know is that Madonna had moved to Miami, another bad move. All she wants now is the money out of her real estate investment, a hilltop castle once owned by mob boss Bugsy Siegel and once used as a private casino.

For "the players" in Hollywood, a good address is the narrow stretch of Pacific Coast Highway leading to Malibu, or the Malibu Colony. The very rich prefer walled-in neighborhoods with security guards and Doberman, or else they move farther and farther away from Los Angeles, into neighborhoods where mountains hide them from the world, like Hidden Valley in the northwest San Fernando Valley.

It is the first warm day of the summer. The Pacific haze is finally lifting, and I am driving through the studioland to meet my agent. In this stretch of Los Angeles, motels are painted pink and purple, with neon signs advertising fortune tellers in their lobby windows. Mexican men are waiting at street corners, hoping to be picked up for construction work, and there is a lot of it since the January 1994 earthquake.

In the middle of Culver City is the old MGM Studios, stretched out like an old whore across the basin, with its water tower still intact. On Overland Boulevard, a street of squat bungalows and auto-repair shops, I come to the "west end" of the lot, with new office buildings and a magnificent wrought-iron gate. Signs proclaiming Tri-Star Pictures. Sony Entertainment. Just like in the movies.

There is a marvelous feeling going on a studio lot. A sense that anything can be achieved. That somehow fate steps in when your name is on a list and the guard ushers you through. I remember when I was only twenty years old, newly arrived, and working on a film. I had one line; we were filming at the big soundstage at MGM, considered the largest in the world. I walked in and—it was magnificent, with huge klieg lights and catwalks. It even smelled like Hollywood.

But to get to that one special moment where you think, This is it, it's going to happen, you have to wade through a swamp of agents and casting directors, acting teachers and photographers, and, finally, the acceptance of your own self. There are an enormous amount of untalented people in Hollywood who keep being rejected and keep hoping. This will never change, and the air sometimes becomes tragic and suffocating. Even if you aren't famous, someone here is making money off you.

At the Peninsula Hotel in Beverly Hills, I meet with my agent for breakfast. It is nine A.M., and we are discussing the fate of my three screenplays, which I wrote five years ago. One has been optioned anew, two are "dancing" with the big boys at various studios.

I lead the screenwriter's life. I have my swimming pool, a lover, and I lunch at the Polo Lounge, at Shutters on the beach in Santa Monica, or at Art's Deli in Studio City, where everyone from Sharon Stone to Danny DeVito eats. I meet with directors and famous stars who have read my work. I smile, but I offer no ideas for free.

The Peninsula is a serious hotel; very expensive, a lot of silver orchids and hothouse roses, and beige. My agent excuses himself to place a call. I sip my orange juice.

I have been debating how to tell my agent we must separate. He's not getting me the money I'd hoped for, and spends a little too much time at his beach house watching sunsets and waiting to hear back from executives who never call back. Sort of a Hollywood purgatory. I've been schmoozed, wined and dined by several agents at very powerful firms who've promised me the world. And I'm going to take one of them up on it.

I think how when you first come to Hollywood it's quite impossible to get an agent. Somehow, you meet someone, you fall through the cracks and you get an agent after a few years. Then suddenly you don't want that agent anymore. You want somebody better.

I know all about false promises, dirty deals and the death of friendship. I'm a little tougher than I used to be. I think to myself, I'll wind this down, I'll sign a contract with the new agent in about a month. I won't tell my current agent any of this, of course, until the last minute. But for now, I'll put on a Hollywood smile, and when he comes back we'll discuss new restaurants, good wines from Northern California, and who's interested in my work at Miramax. And this time around, I'll pick up the check.

At the next table I listen in on a conversation among four men. They are all dressed in sports clothes, gold Rolexes, Armani glasses with eighteen-karat gold wire frames.

You can tell they are agents: The slight tan. The short hair, lightly oiled, cut at Christophe or Umberto in Beverly Hills. They are not eating eggs or meat, just fresh fruit and muffins, coffee, maybe a side of lox. They are, as I will learn later, from the famous William Morris Agency.

"Ovitz was brilliant not to take Seagram's offer," a short man says, biting into a bran muffin. Another man takes a pill out of a small gold box.

"My ulcer. Louise found me unconscious in the bathtub a month ago, bleeding." He sips a glass of milk.

"Sorry about that," all three of his co-workers say quickly, their voices uninterested.

"Wonder how Moloney's taking it." They are discussing Jay Moloney, one of the Young Turk agents at CAA, who fully expects to take over CAA when Ovitz departs for Disney. Now he has a chance.

"Fuck 'im. Who cares? You know damn well what a pain in the ass he is. And the rest of them." The short man makes his point, grabbing a bagel. The table becomes silent, and he looks over at me. I look down at my plate and realize I have ordered an extra large pork sausage, two fried eggs and sliced tomatoes. Suddenly I feel very un–Hollywood.

"So what you think of *Rib Cage?*" an older man at the table, with silver hair, a goatee and a cream Italian suit, asks, putting down his fork.

"It sucks," another man says. "But I could see Paramount taking it, with a rewrite. Right there you're looking at a mil-five. Then if you get two decent stars inhouse, we might be looking at twenty mil." He is talking about twenty million dollars.

These are not production costs. Agents only deal in talent: writers, stars, directors. This is only the cost of getting "bankable" talent.

"Who's the writer?" the little man asks. The old man answers.

"Nobody. Just a jerk. One of my clients."

I wonder if my agent discusses me this way. I eat all my pork sausage.

"Then give it a go. That's good money."

In Hollywood, good money is whatever money is in your pocket for the least amount of work. An agent takes ten to fifteen percent of a star's salary. If a star is making ten million dollars for a film, that agent will pick up a cool million if the film is made. To get the star to say yes, figure five to ten phone calls, dinner and promises.

Agents are as powerful as studio executives because they are experts at the art of influence. CAA is famous for package deals, as is William Morris. An agent can tell a star to say no to a studio, raise his or her price, make demands. Agents have enormous power now that the studio *system* is no longer in operation. Agents hold the honeypot.

I realize I have just been privy to life and death,

twenty million dollars, career and hatred. Just a couple of guys having fun over breakfast in the perfumed air of the Peninsula Hotel.

Heads nod around their table. Calculators are brought out to see who will get what. The thought of commissions on twenty million dollars brings a rosy blush to their faces. This is good money.

The consensus is decided.

LUNCH AT
HARRY WINSTON

If Audrey Hepburn had breakfast at Tiffany's, then I could, at least, lunch at Harry Winston. In 1996, stumbling around Rodeo Drive at dawn in long black gloves, sipping coffee and staring into jewelry store windows, will get you locked up. (All for nothing too, as the merchants use photos in their windows at night.) But lunch, with Italian sandwiches from Il Moro and a smile on my face, lunch makes sense. This is a once-in-a-lifetime situation. Do not try this on your own.

While waiting for an afternoon matinee at the Sherman Oaks Galleria, my friend Debra Devin, a magnificent blonde, insisted we visit Zale's so she could get her gold bracelet cleaned. For free. I commented how attractive several rings in the showcase were, and Debra sniffed, "You don't want those, Donald. That's *beginner's jewelry.*"

Harry Winston's jewels are definitely not for beginners. If Los Angeles is a pot-of-gold town, then along with certain stretches of Malibu sand, Eisner's private telephone number and the latest Bentley, Harry Winston ranks just about at the top of life's ultimates. The jackpot. The place you go to when you're *that* rich.

Rodeo Drive's appeal, for me, diminished as the Eighties finally withered into a mean-spiritedness that marked the beginning of the Nineties. I expect the trappings of wealth to be a sudden cliché, but Harry Winston is booming. I realize this as I walk past a group of well-dressed women ogling a 27-carat, $2.5 million pear-shaped blue-white diamond in Winston's tiny window, past the security guards and sleek Asian woman in the marble entry room, past glass cases set into the wall with sapphires the size of my fist, glittering in Winston's tiny, gray and white atelier.

"We maintain a discreet attitude about our clientele," notes Armand Galvan Espinola, of the Rodeo Drive Harry Winston. "We have an international crowd; the Saudis and Japanese are our biggest customers. Americans too! It's not all oil billionaires and film stars. There are quite a few regular, successful businesspeople who buy at Winston. They've done well, they want beautiful things."

One does not press one's nose against the glass at Harry Winston; jewels are shown to you on a French table covered in black suede. There is a definite erotic charge to this jewelry; it signifies success and beauty and, most of all, power.

"Many of our most important and enthusiastic buyers are men. They're fascinated by the big diamonds," says Espinola with a sly grin. Of course, this is the ultimate trophy, the "you'll never get bigger than this" gauge of success. If a diamond at Harry Winston is going for $5 million—or $14 million in the case of Winston's 34.25-carat, emerald-cut pink diamond—*that* is what you pay. *In cash*. This isn't buying a house. No down payment. No thirty-year mortgage.

Then there is the moment when Winston's jewels are brought out: the sharp intake of breath, the racing heartbeat, the sheer dazzle. I try on that 27-carat diamond and it runs the length of my little finger. Its light blinds. I ask to see some of the big stones, and suddenly $18 million worth of rings, bracelets, brooches and necklaces are swiftly, precisely laid in front of me. I need oxygen. I feel dizzy, but I feel *good*.

The term "precious jewels" covers only diamonds, emeralds, rubies, sapphires and true pearls. The best rubies are from Burma; emeralds, Colombia; and sapphires, Kashmir. Diamonds are not only from DeBeers in South Africa; they are mined all over the world, including the United States.

In the more important pieces, I am stunned by the intensity of color. A square-cut, 23-carat fancy yellow diamond ring, at about $500,000.00, has a yellow like wings of a baby canary. A cushion-cut, 15-carat Burmese ruby ring, surrounded by diamonds and priced at $2.5 million, has an electric, stoplight red that makes the stone seem alive.

"These stones are among the finest in the world," Espinola remarks quietly. "They are in a league of their own. All diamonds from Harry Winston are cut at our Fifth Avenue headquarters; you buy the work of stone cutters, polishers and other artisans, including our principal designer, Ambaji Shinde, who's been with the firm over thirty years. For these people, these stones are their life's work."

It takes up to six months studying a major rough diamond to decide where to make the first cut, and months to cut it, when the diamond goes "on the spool." Harry Winston, during the middle of this century, had an uncommon talent for understanding how a diamond could be cut from the rough. Harry Winston *understood* diamonds, period.

As a poet, I understand how certain passions in life are unexplainable and without coherent defense. I am fascinated with the diamonds that have their own names and histories and cost more than small islands in the South Pacific; these make me weep.

When Diana Vreeland, as editor of *Vogue* in the Sixties, wanted to photograph a major diamond, the first person she called was Harry Winston.

"He knew I had this *beguine* for diamonds," Vreeland stated in her book *Allure*. "I went, and this time I saw it, a 65-carat marquise. It was *this* thick; as you know, thickness is everything in a stone. It isn't a thing of lust for me . . . it's love. When I see diamonds in a north light, on a little velvet pillow . . . I *die*. 'Oh, Mr. Winston,' I said, 'you really *got* something here!' "

Harry Winston and Los Angeles seem to go hand in hand; here there is Hollywood, enormous wealth from the Pacific Rim and the Middle East, and the glamour sensibility that Los Angeles is desperately trying to hold on to.

"Not surprising all those jewels go to Middle Eastern women," huffs a girlfriend of mine with two children and a somewhat dull vision of what constitutes fantasy and reality. "After all, no one in Los Angeles has that kind of money anymore."

Not true. The money is still being spent. Winston is notoriously generous in letting celebrities borrow their jewels for the Oscars and other events. Even Sharon Stone showed she could be "seduced" by Winston's jewels, stating that she "thought" Harry Winston had "given" her the jewelry. The jewelry was returned after some unattractive press. Nice try, Sharon, but no cigar.

A retired film actress whom I know too well sighs when I mention Harry Winston.

"The best. Nothing finer. I just wonder how many of these new girls in the business actually buy those jewels. In the days of Paulette Goddard and Elizabeth Taylor, stars *owned* their jewels. Let's face it, most of these girls today just can't carry it off. Their faces are too vulgar."

I think of a story that went around Hollywood in the late Seventies. Sir Lew Grade and Francis Coppola were both on their respective yachts. Coppola shouted out, "My boat's bigger than yours!" to which Sir Lew Grade shouted back, "Yes, but I *own* mine!"

Part of the erotic charge of these fabulous jewels is the danger. They can inspire murder, robbery, lies, kidnapping and bad luck (as in the legend of the famous Hope Diamond, which Winston purchased from Evalyn Walsh McLean's estate in 1949 and donated to the Smithsonian). At the same time, they take your breath away.

Insurance companies send out guards to protect certain pieces. Another status symbol in Hollywood: You have guards because you are famous and you have even more guards because of your *jewels.*

"When I was filming *Scenes from the Class Struggle in Beverly Hills,* Jacqueline Bisset and I wore jewels from Harry Winston," remembers cult film star Mary Woronov. "Bisset had the rubies and diamonds, I had the emeralds. Because of insurance, a security guard went *where* my emeralds *went.* If I went to the toilet, he stood outside the door. If I was changing in the dressing room, he was in there with me. These guys are totally unabashed, and they carry big guns."

The great, legendary jewels always seem to have passed through the house of Harry Winston, now run by his son, Ronald Winston, since 1978. Harry Winston has held more than sixty of the world's 303 major diamonds, more than any other jeweler, government or royalty.

It was Winston who cut and sold the Taylor-Burton Diamond, at 69.42 carats; the Lal Quila, a 72.76-carat green diamond sold to King Farouk of Egypt which has since disappeared; and the Star of the East, a 94.80-carat pear-shaped diamond sold recently at Harry Winston for over $10 million. Winston has sold diamonds like the Star of Sierra Leone, an emerald-cut 32.53 carats, or the Niarchos Diamond, a 128.25-carat D-flawless pear-shaped diamond; truly huge, utterly spellbinding.

Diamonds have a fascinating way of passing through different hands and developing their own history, pedigree and romance. With Winston's jewels, you pass into another kind of history; you become part of the stone's ultimate story. It is the only story in the world where an inanimate object commands such scrupulous attention and thorough record.

Fabulous jewels are not politically correct. The pious will always be trying to tell us how to spend money, what to do with our lives. It is only because their lives haven't turned out the way they hoped, and the successful generally pay for it.

Precious, high-quality jewels are their own market, a guaranteed investment, and have been used as collateral on loans, down payments on property, stock trades. The world of serious diamonds is, and always has been, a closed one, particularly in Los Angeles and New York, where you literally have to be born into a diamond family to get into the business. Not unlike Hollywood.

At Harry Winston on Rodeo Drive, I have lunch with Armand and try on a ruby and diamond bracelet with 34 rubies totaling 35 carats, and 158 diamonds totaling 28 carats. Then I try on a V-shaped diamond necklace that converts into a bracelet and a comparative bargain at $250,000.00.

"I shall never, ever be quite this rich," I sigh above the shimmer.

"Winston has a full catalog of more reasonably priced jewelry," Espinola says, trying to somehow comfort me.

"What is the least I can buy?" I ask, realizing I suddenly sound desperately not famous, not rich.

Espinola shows me the price of admission: an 18K gold chain, quite nice really, at $1,200.00. A gold-plated writing pen for $800.00 and a gold and titanium keyring for $680.00. I then see the Harry Winston whistle, with jewels, in 18K gold, at a little over $6,000.00.

I could be persuaded to accept a $6,000.00 whistle as a gift, of course, but after the millions of dollars of jewels slithering around my neck and arms, it seems so . . . average. At this moment I realize it is time for me to exit, to leave the fantasy and go back to the San Fernando Valley. Reality must come back to me, somehow, or I shall be lost forever.

I turn and look at Armand Espinola.

"Can I see that 27-carat diamond one more time?" I ask sweetly, masking a breaking heart.

"Of course," he says.

I slip it on my little finger and hold it up to a north light. It's quite heavy, and it seems to have its own energy, a whispering, brilliantly faceted energy. I remind myself that I have just had lunch at Harry Winston, and I believe in ultimates. I believe in glamour, in danger. I believe in diamonds, held up to the light, that make me cry.

LITTLE GHOSTS

There is a place, beyond Los Angeles, where dreams are simple. I drive through sliced, yellowing mountains to get there, past Soledad Canyon and the Vasquez Rocks, past the skeletons of new Spanish-style homes, their red clay tiles still bundled and stacked on roofs. They are clustered in the hundreds near highway exits and on flattened mountaintops. Beyond them are hills easily ignited, and signs predicting how many more miles it will take to get to the high desert. Suddenly, at this new, higher altitude, I can see only opaque sky, and I disappear into the cream haze of the Antelope Valley.

I am here to listen to the wind, and to ghosts. There are over fourteen little ghosts in the Antelope Valley. In this high desert infants and small children have been murdered by their parents and guardians at a rate, according to the *Los Angeles Times,* that is three times higher than the Los Angeles County average, placing it among the highest in the United States. I am here because the beatings and murders have not stopped or diminished. More little ghosts are on their way.

Some of the victims have names. Others didn't last a day. In each of the most violent cases, methamphetamine use was attributed to the victim's parents or guardians. Many of the ghosts are baby and toddler girls, with names like Briana Lee, Deedra and Sabreena, names that echo a particular fantasy sensibility of their mothers. These are the names of high romance, of a dream state, a place their mothers wish they could be.

These are also the names appearing like beads on thread, linking methamphetamine and violence. These simple dreams no longer work, here at the end of the century, at the beginning of the Mojave Desert, where everything is new, hopeful, and washed by dry wind.

Here the nameless include a newborn son, murdered by his parents, who wrapped his body in a plastic bag and threw it in a Dumpster. Or another infant, strangled at birth and kept in a plastic bag in its mother's bedroom while she decided what to do with it. The decision took most of the day.

Then there are the girls. Here, in the fixed and hallucinatory sun, thirteen-month-old Briana Lee Schmidt was shaken to death by her mother's boyfriend, Robert Patalasky. The act of shaking can produce, in an infant, heart trauma, breakages in the spine, damage to internal organs, and a snapping of the neck. Briana had been hospitalized six weeks earlier, but her injuries had not been ruled child abuse. Patalasky is now facing the death penalty, because Briana Lee Schmidt was not just shaken to death but raped and sodomized as well.

Deedra Hunter was four years old when she was beaten to death by her parents, Richard Leach and Michelle Hunter. Deedra was a pretty little girl, according to the examiners at the county coroner's office. She was ready for a small world, one with limits. Upon discovery, Deedra's corpse was covered with major bruises, cuts and human bite marks. Deedra's two-year-old stepbrother had similar injuries, but he survived. Both Leach and Hunter pleaded no contest to second-degree murder and were sentenced to fifteen years to life in state prison.

In the case of Sabreena Przybyszewski, the nuance between malicious intent and accident blur. Sabreena died at the age of five months. Unlike her parents, Christopher Daugherty and Elizabeth Przybyszewski, Sabreena had blue eyes. At the time of Sabreena's death, Daugherty was estranged from Sabreena's mother, Elizabeth; and even though the couple had problems, Elizabeth left Sabreena in Christopher's care. It was only two days; Sabreena was later pronounced dead from chronic physical abuse and methamphetamine poisoning. Her body had evidence, although healing, of twelve rib fractures, bruised wrists, a burned leg, scarred feet, and swelling on all appendages. Daugherty was sentenced to eleven years in state prison; Elizabeth was sentenced to one year in county jail under a plea bargain that she was a passive participant.

At the time of death Sabreena measured twenty-one inches long and weighed in at fourteen pounds. She had been, according to Daugherty, a heavy breather—not surprising with twelve rib fractures—and when he couldn't hear her breathing he decided to call 911. Sabreena Przybyszewski was buried by the Chapel of the Valley in Palmdale. As she was an infant, her casket, manufactured by the Westwood Casket Company in San Bernardino County, measured just twenty-four inches and was octagonal, with a pink exterior. It is, apparently, a very popular model.

Patalasky, Leach, Hunter, Daugherty and Przybyszewski were all methamphetamine users. At the time of their arrests, Patalasky was twenty-three years old; Richard Leach, twenty-six; Michelle Hunter, twenty-five; Christopher Daugherty was thirty-two. Elizabeth Przybyszewski was only twenty-one. Daugherty lived in Littlerock and Leach and Hunter lived in Palmdale, Patalasky in Lancaster. Palmdale and Lancaster are the twin cities of the high desert, stretching out into a flat, astonishingly open valley that absorbs the colors of sunsets and windblown grit. There is no real place where Palmdale ends and Lancaster begins. The majority of residents here are white, several shades darker than the Mojave sand. And like the fluid stretch of their neighborhoods. There is no singular definition of what makes up a local killer. Some of them are poor, living in pressboard shacks on uncharted roads past Littlerock and Newberry Springs. Others are middle class and the sons and daughters of the middle class. Some migrated here for construction work, others were raised here. They live in tract houses with greenhouse windows in the kitchen, or in condominiums with vaulted ceilings and mountain views. Still others live in trailer parks with neatly tended playgrounds and miniature cactus gardens. Suddenly there are monsters next door.

I realize, as I park my car next to an abandoned, half-built subdivision that has already been torched and is now a blackened graph, that we become frightened when we see traces of ourselves in the killers. The comfort of our identity is twisted by something beyond our control; a certain sense of assault develops in the mirror we choose to look into. And, like the remains of this particular three-bedroom, two-bath dream, the victims will be forgotten when new money pours in; there will be no color to our bankruptcies, no chill in abandonment. Things have happened too fast in the high desert. The land is warning us.

I speak to a woman who is a clerk in the Antelope Valley court system about the Daughterty-Przybyszewski case.

"Oh yeah. I remember that guy," she says quietly. "He was an animal."

This is one of the first real conversations I have. People here decline conversations about the child abuse and murders in their desert. It is as though I am asking about them, and I am not. As if their desert's become tainted and they don't want anyone to know. I realize this is a family place. Family secrets can take decades to uncover.

"From what I understand, Elizabeth Przybyszewski showed remorse at her hearing," I say guardedly.

"That girl's a drug addict," the woman snaps. "And besides, you know remorse is just a lawyer's gimmick."

I think of Elizabeth, who completed her sentence and a drug-rehabilitation program and has since moved away. She will have to deal with precisely this attitude wherever she goes, if people know. She will have to learn secrecy, new definitions of truth. She will have to look into her mirror and wipe away the assault.

The woman continues. "There's no explaining these

people. Read the reports. Read what they did. And they're everywhere, here."

"Is it the desert?" I ask. "The geographic isolation?"

"What isolation? Palmdale's a big place. There's lots to do."

"You tell me," I counter.

"It's methamphetamine," the woman replies without hesitation. "The drug people that wind up here, a lot of them are hicks, serious Appalachia types, they know they wouldn't last too long in L.A. The high desert's an easy place to get in and out of. There's always Vegas, Bakersfield. . . . Rumor has it, once out of Camarillo, they give the child molesters a one-way bus ticket to the Antelope Valley. And you know, I believe it."

The Antelope Valley is the last bedroom community Los Angeles will ever have to offer. There is no more horizon, and no more Shangri-La. Before Palmdale was a city, it was a dot in the desert called Palmenthal and Harold. It was the terrain of the Kitanemuk Indians, who hunted wild antelope; hence the name Antelope Valley. White settlers brought alfalfa, pears and apples, the major source of industry until World War II. Many did not prosper, as the area was plagued—quite typical of California—with drought, unscrupulous land developers and a general ignorance of survival tactics necessary to the western landscape.

In the Fifties the defense and aerospace industries came here, bringing with them the Southern California dream, based on affordable housing, supermarkets and the knowledge that work would be plentiful for years to come. This was the same basis for other suburbs, like Torrance and Lakewood.

Land was, and still is, cheap. And there is a lot of it in the high desert. By the 1980s Palmdale and Lancaster had become giant suburbs, with enormous housing tracts built by Kaufman and Broad and their imitators. Prices for homes were in the low eighties, nineties and hundreds, prices unheard of in the Los Angeles basin. Neighborhoods now have their own front entrances with the suggestion of gates and romantic names in affluent script, like Moonshadows, St. Laurent and Fiesta. Avenues are labeled alphabetically on a simple grid that is very clean when seen by air. This is ideal for builders who prefer to chart their investments by plane or helicopter, never touching down. Drives have Spanish names. It is exact Southern California synthesis, without narrative, or soul.

This region is conservative in a way only a young suburban community can be; to attract commerce. Words like "gay," "lesbian," "multiracial" and "multicultural" have no significance here. The word "multiplex" does.

In 1950 there were 16,084 inhabitants in the Antelope Valley. In 1990 the number was 250,510 citizens and growing. During Tom Bradley's tenure, an airport, the Palmdale International Airport, was planned. Land was bought up by speculators and resold. But the imaginary airport is still being planned. And near this land are shacks without addresses or roads. And methamphetamine labs in secluded ranches once used for horse breeding.

Here you work for a big firm, now mostly construction, buy your first house and have lots of children, drive dirt bikes in the desert and through parched canyons, shoot guns out in the flats, picnic at Lake Hughes. This is, as one Encino Realtor joked with me, the last great breeding ground of Southern California.

Here the desert becomes metallic and wicked during the late afternoon and cold at night. Residents speak of the valley's beauty. Also the strength and severity of its weather, with intense dust storms, high winds and flash floods. But here you can see the key, and it is a 360-degree cage, enveloping the cities with a livid, pale heart. All of this for only five thousand dollars down and a one-hour drive from Burbank.

Residents also insist this is a good place to raise a family; churches are tightly knit, schools well funded and clean. The citizens speak in a Pete Wilson, we-play-by-the-rules sort of way. The words "permit," "zoning" and "airport" are part of the high desert vocabulary. As well as the words "child murder" and "methamphetamine." That is blamed on all these new people, kids having kids, a general restlessness that never used to be here. But no one sees the rattlesnake under the tree, awake in the shade. And coiled.

I am having lunch at Karen's Corner on Palmdale Boulevard. I had tried to find a shady spot to park, but there is no shade in the high desert, only shadows. It is 99° outside and I am listening to Garth Brooks on the jukebox. On the walls around me are stuffed bass the owner caught at Lake Isabella. These prize winners, with vulgar lips and fat sides, have been preserved by an unusually dedicated taxidermist and are mounted on shellacked manzanita branches all over the restaurant's side walls and in custom glass cases in the back.

Around me are families, the men wearing clean pressed clothes, with unkempt beards and baseball caps with the logos of cement firms and lumber yards. The children are quiet. The babies lay somnambulistically in plastic child hampers. Their mothers chat amiably with their sisters-in-law and girlfriends who happen to be having lunch with them. The men are surprisingly quiet around their women, and stiff. Yet at a table near me, five men sit together, drinking coffee and smoking cigarettes between their thumb and forefinger, and their conversation is animated. Jokes are being told. Innuendo abounds.

Turning back to the families, I notice one couple with an infant, and they look like Christopher Daugherty and Elizabeth Przybyszewski. The young man stares straight ahead and the mother's eyes are bloodshot. She smokes cigarette after cigarette, and when her baby cries she bounces it up and down on her lap a little too hard. I suddenly feel terrified. It can't be them. This much I know. But these people could have been them.

I think about Elizabeth and Christopher, and how their photographs show two attractive young white kids. Christopher is staring into the police lens with wide eyes and a handsome, baby face. Elizabeth has almond-shaped eyes, a sensual and all-American face, with flower hair. Her eyes just miss the lens.

Something is wrong here, I advise myself. They look so nice. Like the couple at the booth in front of me. It is then I know our horrors, for the most part, are invisible, having already taken place when we finally see evidence. In child abuse, when bruises can be seen, it means the child has been beaten on a regular basis. By the time the parent is staring into the police lens, the rattlesnake has left the shade of its tree. The child is dead.

This is the wild, sad heat that stays in my veins. I keep wondering at what moment, what lousy Tuesday night, actual corruption begins in the psyche. The kind of corruption that leads to death. Methamphetamine is blamed for the most violent of murders, but there are other factors, including poverty, ignorance, stress and evil, if evil is allowed in today's rhetoric. Perhaps evil blossoms in wide open space, in sand and rocks, inducing a dream state, the same dream state that allows baby girls to be named Deedra and Sabreena and Briana Lee. It is the most human of states. To want to feel good, feel better, or not feel at all.

Consider the reality.

It is February 20, 1992, and a cold day in Littlerock, California. The mountains and sands are wet from February's intense rains, which have turned the San Fernando Valley in the south into an emergency zone. Here there has been flooding and slides.

At 4:38 A.M. Bryan Riley and Lloyd Teel respond to a child not breathing call. When they get there, they discover a female infant lying on a dining-room table, in a house in front of Christopher M. Daugherty's fifth-wheel trailer. This is where he has been taking care of Sabreena. The woman who resides in the front house is there, with Christopher, who is attempting CPR on the infant. All the lights in the house are on.

Dawn is still an hour and a half away. The air is bitten with a watery February cold, the kind that stays in bones. The two deputies observe the victim lying on the dining table on her back with her head pointing south and her feet pointing north. She is not breathing, and her feet are cold to the touch. Daugherty, assisted by another deputy who arrived earlier, continues CPR.

When we are victims, it is reported what direction we are found in at the time of death. Our heads point north or south, our feet possibly east. Our hands could be stretched toward the Pacific. Or the Rockies. This is our last concise act of being.

Elizabeth Przybyszewski is contacted and is en route. When she arrives she becomes hysterical. Later, at Palmdale Hospital, Dr. Fagan in Emergency contacts the two deputies and advises them that the victim, Sabreena, has bruises and scratches and cuts that may be attributed to child abuse. Upon examining Sabreena, Riley and Teel observe "a reddish bruised area along the victim's left shin, running from her knee to the ankle, a small injury, scabbed over on the top of her left foot, possibly a burn, a scar 1/2" long, just below the lower lip, a bruised area 1" in diameter on the left ear . . . redness and swelling on both wrists, scars and blisters on both feet, possible injury to the anal orifice."

On an infant twenty-one inches in length, a half-inch scar below the lower lip takes up most of the chin. A bruise an inch in diameter on the left ear is at least half the ear.

At this point the officers feel a child abuse investigation is warranted. Now, at the age of twenty-one, Elizabeth is being questioned and read her rights. Christopher is in a haze. Both parents give conflicting answers when questioned. A burn came about "because the baby was left too close to a fire and briefly forgotten." Elizabeth's answers are fairly concise. Christopher's answers are vague. Both parents are taken into custody.

The police report attesting to these events ends with the following observation [emphasis added]: "The suspect [Daugherty] seemed indifferent about the incident when asked when he would go to the hospital. *He stated he would get there when he could.*"

Speed freaks handle their children roughly because they are not aware they are being rough. Methamphetamine poisoning killed Sabreena. Daugherty's trailer was full of meth dust. All it took was a baby's fingers to touch the dust. Then those tiny fingers reach, naturally, for the mouth. Meth stayed around Sabreena, circling like an invisible plasma. It pulsed through the hands that shook her too hard, left her too close to a fire and then forgot about her. When the drug finally got inside her, when her heart stopped beating and she lay facedown in her crib, the drug had won.

I have just finished attending a Narcotics Anonymous meeting at the Desert Community Church on Avenue J, in Lancaster. It is a clear, warm night, and in the parking lot I speak with a recovering methamphetamine addict. Her name, for now, is Debbie. Debbie has had two abortions and two marriages, both to methamphetamine users. She now lives alone. I ask her if she knows about the murders.

"Sure. But that's old news," she says in a soft voice.

Her reactions are slow. She lights a cigarette and studies me.

"I want to know what methamphetamine is like. Was like for you. Be a poet, Debbie, and tell me."

Debbie smiles. As she speaks, I look up at the sky. The stars are out and pulsing. I have never seen so many stars.

"Things vibrate. And you feel good. Things are silver and gold. You feel important and sexy. You feel like everything is exciting. How's that?" she asks innocently. I nod my head and she decides to continue.

"Snorting is okay. But you get higher if you shoot up."

"What about coming down?" I ask.

"You don't want to come down from crank. That's for sure. It's the worst. So you don't." Debbie flicks her cigarette into the night, and the warm wind blows her pale brown hair around her face. I shiver because I suddenly understand. I could be high up here too, under these glistening stars, with the warm wind, the silences, the dark roads. But they are the same silences I found among the married men in Karen's Corner. Only vacancies to be filled with something. Methamphetamine is the drug of choice in the high desert. It makes the desert seem fast and understandable. But the desert is the catalyst. Here it is easy to be seduced.

It runs about twenty-five thousand dollars to start up a meth lab, ruling out the possibility that while methamphetamine is the poor man's cocaine, the poor man can make it at home. The high desert is ideal for the drug's manufacture: Due to open terrain, you can see the cops coming, and you can hide the stink. Methamphetamine has a distinct chemical odor as it is being made. It needs air.

Here methamphetamine's distribution is indicative of what is happening throughout suburban and rural America. Drug-manufacturing organizations are set up in minimally populated regions. Overhead is low. Things are quiet, and business is good. This is precisely the same attitude that fits into any small-town chamber of commerce.

Violent crimes related to methamphetamine have increased here to such an extent that residents and police have taken different responsible measures. One result is the Children's Center of the Antelope Valley. Esther Gillies, its director, has developed and expanded the center's sex-abuse programs to include a task force for identification of abuse; through diagnosis the community can realize which claims are real.

"There are many kinds of sexual and physical abuse," Gillies explains. "Parental, sibling, outside . . . Parents go through complete devastation when they find out, for example, that their child has been molested by an outside influence. In the most severe cases, the most brutal . . . Yes, in the Antelope Valley, methamphetamine plays a role in these deaths. . . . You must remember, this is a conservative community. It is fecund ground for things to go awry."

Gillies's last statement startles me. She continues in a measured, highly intelligent voice.

"The boom is over. Money is tight or there's no money at all. The winds start in September and blow for months. Sometimes highways are closed down, due to dust storms. Beyond the cities, there are houses and shacks where children are living, and we can't find the road in."

Deedra, Sabreena and Briana Lee were not killed in the middle of nowhere but in average neighborhoods. But I can see other children, walking down dirt roads to the highway. They are used to the sound of wind and their parents. There is meth dust on the carpet. There are hypodermic needles in the kitchen. And the television is on, very, very low.

It is appalling to realize we are capable of addiction to a drug whose main ingredient, acetone, can be bought in any hardware store. Our biological propensity for ingesting poisons is unequaled.

Psychiatrist and psychoanalyst Lee B. Gold, an associate clinical professor of psychiatry at USC, points out that "methamphetamine has no brains. The impact is on mood. If substance abusers can't change externally, they try to feel better internally; to get away from something that's subjectively painful. Either way, they're trying to dispose of their own image. They don't want to see themselves."

Listening to Dr. Gold, I think of metamorphosis. How wings break through a papery cocoon, exposing a chrysalis to air. Or how a killer is made. Prolonged methamphetamine use makes skin gaunt. Fingernails go brown, come off. There is hair and teeth loss. After the rush and shimmer, after weeks to years of little or no sleep, the drug provokes an obvious psychosis, with rage, paranoia, oversensitive reactions to sounds. The kind infants and toddlers make. Violence doesn't relieve the tension. Eyes become old and dry. And the mirror has gone sour.

"In this self-centered world," Dr. Gold explains, "pleasure must come on an immediate basis. Drug use is increased to get the effect remembered. Sex is part of this pleasure. But if an addicted couple have an unwanted child, it may be viewed as an interference, an intruder on the daily high. This implication of self-indulgence, of the avoidance of subjective feelings of pain, leads to a sense of the moment, without giving thought to the consequences."

I wonder what it takes, physically, to hit a child. Or throw an infant against a wall. Or sodomize it. Very little energy, less than pushing a stalled car out of an intersection. I ask Dr. Gold if the high desert attracts addicts and ultimately leads to violence.

"Substance abuse may seek isolation because of a paucity inside. I make generic statements for a reason. Without data, I can't be specific. Then it's known as wild analysis."

In this decade of white-trash glamour we are no longer surprised by shotgun murders in trailer parks, religious fanaticism, or incest of exceptionally varied nuance and drama, but when an infant is murdered by its parents the facts become transcendent, beyond what is now "average" news. Joan Didion has stated that "the imposition of a sentimental, or false, narrative on the disparate and often random experiences that constitute the life of a city, or country, means, necessarily, that much of what happens in that city or country will be rendered merely

illustrative, a series of set pieces, or performance op-
portunities."

This is true. In the high desert, stating that child murder is epidemic would be like stating Alzheimer's is epidemic to Sun City or St. Petersburg, Florida. What we
are looking at are Didion's set pieces, the horrors pre-
sented in the arresting landscape of the high desert,
making it almost cinematic and, therefore, in Southern
California, wholly understandable. These set pieces are
not the result of a false narrative but of a poetic one.
Drugs and dreams. And I begin to understand wild
analysis. Here in the high desert, it is a misery, still sen-
tient, shimmering with vacancies and silences, and it is
killing its young.

I decide to attend the Antelope Valley Fair. Held at the
end of August, before those September winds, each day
of the fair salutes a different community, from Palmdale
to Leona Valley.

In the peach and vermilion dusk, when the rides light
up and Reba McEntire's unit is turning up the amps,
getting ready for her to sing, I walk around. This is a
place for the American core. In the parking lot, motorcycles and trucks are parked in precise, neat rows. And
their paint is new.

Everywhere I look there are children: on the streets
of Palmdale and Lancaster; in cars on the highway, their
arms stretched out of backseat windows to feel the
wind; here at the fair with cotton-candy stains on their
necks. And they belong to this landscape, as much a
part of it as the mountains and sun. Los Angeles has

gotten too old, too sly. Children were never part of the
landscape, and never will be.

I suddenly picture Los Angeles, with its boulevards to
the Pacific, lined with flowers blooming in electric, easy
to understand colors, seldom lasting a day. They are
planned not to last, like the babies of the Antelope Valley. If Los Angeles is our postcard, now burned at the
edges, then its suburbs are only distilled into a lighter
color, and magnified under a larger sky. This is the danger of growing hybrids: the scentless bedroom communities with easy to understand dreams, surrounded by
wind and dust, bordered by the chalk outlines of high
desert lots where new homes will be built. It is the
same chalk used to outline a corpse on a dining-room
table or in a crib.

Here children are the point, the main ingredient, like
acetone for methamphetamine, or barren land for international airports; even the concept, now dead, that
nothing can disrupt a self-contained world. The dream
state becomes clear. The wind carries cancer and corruption. And the desperate have moved in.

RED CANDLE ANNIVERSARY

This recent January 17, I took a lit red Christmas candle, and held it, to remind myself. Exactly two years ago there was an earthquake here in Sherman Oaks that destroyed most of the suburb; I had run out into the darkness, over shards of blown-out windows and partially collapsed ceilings, to see if our neighbors were even alive.

They were alive, sitting in their cars, headlights on, listening to the radio. I was holding a lit red candle, and I ran to various residences, checking, right through the dawn. I was never aware the red candle had dripped all over my hand, covering it in hot wax.

I live in a suburb, Sherman Oaks; five minutes over Benedict Canyon to Beverly Hills. Five minutes over Beverly Glen to Westwood. Five minutes to the Ventura Freeway, or the San Diego Freeway.

My house, that I share with my lover, John, is rambling and elegant and completely walled in. It sits in a heavily wooded area where the hills begin their steep ascent, and it is very, very private. Knowing Los Angeles the way we do, privacy was a key factor.

I know the mantra of real estate agents; my house has been occupied by producers, and writers like me, and will continue to be long after John and I have vacated.

It's one of those kind of houses. I am quick to point out that Lara Flynn Boyle is a block away; Michael Biehn is just a couple of houses up the hill, as is Harry Dean Stanton, recently robbed and beaten in his house by three young Hispanics. I will also mention, in the same breath, that Warren and Annette have finally finished their remodel after the quake, and it looks fabulous. Not that I have been there. I just heard about it.

These are the little points of interest that keep me from thinking about when I was attacked in a supermarket parking lot, then involved in a car collision, a planned car collision, the next day in the same parking lot. A black woman, dressed like Marcia Clark, and quite attractive, screamed directly in my face that she was a lawyer, where was my insurance, she was going to sue. When I said, somewhat groggily from the collision, that it was her fault, she really exploded, demanding a thousand dollars in cash on the spot or she would call the police. I then realized she was scamming me, and told her so. She drove away incredibly fast. Just another day in an upscale suburb.

I remember this because it was two days before the quake. Everyone seemed very tightly wound, bitchy. I remember saying to my friend and editor at the time, Greg Critser, at a lunch in Pasadena, that this was "earthquake weather." His wife, Antoinette, looked at me with wide eyes and whispered, "You know, you might be right."

During the quake, most of the outside walls guarding the house completely collapsed. The house itself rode out the quake, but we lost approximately $50,000 worth of china, crystal and antiques. When the insurance money rolled through four months later, everything was fixed, and our slow dance on the fault line continued.

On the day of the earthquake, when we were huddled next to a battery-operated radio in the kitchen and dreaming of freshly perked coffee, John went into a form of low-grade shock, shivering and staring at me with glazed eyes. I threw my mink coat over him and fixed him a large scotch. He pleaded with me: "I need cigarettes, I've got not one," he said.

"In case you haven't noticed, darling, it's the end of the world outside," I murmured soothingly. "You know, Armageddon. The day we say our prayers. Look out the window. See that glow over Ventura Boulevard? Those are *flames*."

"Please," he said.

If you have ever truly *loved* someone, you know that word means you will battle anything to get it done. It is a frightening word, one that Lillian Hellman almost never used, and a word Dashiell Hammett, the love of her life, never ever used.

Driving out toward Ventura Boulevard, I suddenly felt like Lillian Hellman. I grumbled. I cursed. I was living with an impossible man. I dodged a part of the road that had collapsed and was suddenly on Ventura Boulevard. Six buildings were in flames, two stores were being looted, and water was shooting up from a large pipe that had come up through the street.

People were strolling as if it were Sunday, through the rubble, taking pictures. Others were sitting on the street, crying or screaming for no reason. I drove past a row of six apartment houses that had cracked in half; others had collapsed in on their parking garages. I realized then I live in a city about as stable as a sand dune. It will never stop rebuilding itself from earthquakes, rains, riots, fires. Architecture becomes meaningless. Ditto antiquity, art, propriety, tradition.

But almost everything was meaningless that strange, hot day. I found a liquor store that was open. Its windows were shattered and everything on its shelves, every single item, was on the carpeted floor. The owner was ecstatic about the carpeted floors. He kept mumbling that he didn't lose one bottle of liquor, not one. People were on their hands and knees, looking for things. A woman with stiff blond hair in a Chanel coat and jeans was crawling toward a toppled box of tampons. Others, all on their hands and knees, were shopping for popcorn, nail-polish remover, bagged ice, frozen enchiladas.

"Could I have two packs of Benson and Hedges Deluxe Ultra Lights, regulars?" I asked, my voice sounding suddenly very surreal.

"Of course, sir," the liquor store owner said, getting down on all fours and wading through packs of cigarettes until he found my request.

"That'll be five dollars," he said, rising cheerfully. He should have charged me ten dollars. Or twenty, I thought, amused.

As I walked out of the liquor store, there was an explosion two blocks down. A furniture store's fourteen-foot window shattered, then flames. Fire trucks. A new rumble, a heavy aftershock, perhaps 5.0.

A couple slowed their metallic beige Lexus, rolled down the windows and asked me, "Is that liquor store open?" They were both wearing Giorgio Armani sunglasses. The woman was wearing a crocheted, flowered cloche hat, and talking on a cellular phone. I nodded my head, yes. They stopped their car in the middle of the street, ran into the liquor store, joining the group of shoppers on all fours, like dogs in a garbage dump.

It is this one vision that sustains me. It was noon and 90° F. The sun was shining between rumbles and sirens. I found cigarettes in a war zone; and when I light my anniversary candle and look into the high, white flame, I realize there is only one particular picture of Los Angeles in the Nineties. And it is this: people in Chanel coats, T-shirts and flowered hats and sunglasses, on their hands and knees, searching for tampons, cigarettes and aspirin.

THE SANDBOX

On December 14, 1996, the world premiere for *Evita* was held at the Shrine Auditorium in downtown Los Angeles, an enormous art deco Moorish-Egyptian bonbon with the biggest screen on the West Coast. I have been told over the years in Hollywood that the Shrine was not built with city government money, but handshakes and funds from the big boys at their studios. The big boys wanted a *big* screen to show *big* pictures.

Well, *Evita* is about as *big* a picture as we'll see in the Nineties, with Alan Parker, its director, winding up the true star of this film. This is not to say Madonna is not good; she is utterly flawless. She's not as gutsy or forceful as Elaine Paige or Patti LuPone, but she moves through this huge motion picture with a geisha's grace. She should be congratulated.

My tale begins with a phone call. On the other end of the line is Samantha Dunn, now a journalist with *Premiere* magazine. A breathy, hurried voice.

"Donald, what are you up to tonight?"

"Nothing much," I say flatly.

"How would you like to go to the world premiere of *Evita* and the private party afterward? Can you be ready in twenty minutes? It's black tie, darling."

"I can be ready in twenty minutes, no problem."

My heart is beating wildly. People from Beverly Hills to Santa Monica have been mumbling that this premiere is *the* ticket. And, oh God, *Madonna* will be there. And *Antonio Banderas.*

Outside the Shrine bleachers have been set up to seat up to six or seven thousand people, and they seem full. We are on the long red carpet, just like at the Oscars, and I am listening to Marisa Tomei in front of us exclaiming in wonder, "Isn't this something? Can you believe this? Can you?" to her friend. I want to say "Yes, darling, I can believe this. I still believe in all of this. It is, of course, my downfall."

Photo ops are done with Madonna. The crowd screams, girls in their early twenties are crying, screaming out Madonna's name. Madonna is made up within an inch of her life, and she handles everything quite gracefully.

There is no time you can really get near Madonna; a moving island of international photographers, television crews and filmmakers surrounds her, at some places ten men deep, so she has to walk slowly, otherwise she will trip and fall flat on her face. And of course, her baby's father, that man (No one in town seems to know his name. Mention him and faces go blank. "Is it Mario? No. I think it's Alberto. Carlos? Gustavio? Something like that.") with the rippling muscles and the air of a dance-hall instructor, is showing a lot of gleaming teeth.

Watching this astonishing display I begin to understand what star power entails, what you, of course, have to give up, and also how far you can go.

When interviewed for *Entertainment Tonight,*

Madonna smiles sweetly and says, "I feel like I'm dreaming. I don't think this is really happening."

How coy. In a city of ultimates, Madonna has reached her apex. When you are dealing with something this *big,* not unlike Elizabeth Taylor entering Rome in 1962's *Cleopatra,* there is no looking back. Suddenly a stasis will set in. Other projects just won't seem as important. As *big.*

Samantha and I are seated at a table of agents, and their wives, from Creative Artists Agency. All the men's tuxedos are Gianni Versace; their wives are dressed in strapless black lace ball gowns, or slinky jersey numbers with no brassiere. The wives wear simple jewelry. A ten-carat diamond wedding ring; five-carat diamond ear studs from Harry Winston. Too simple for words, of course.

There is an enormous amount of cleavage at this soiree; breasts are popping out of strapless gowns with perky desperation. In fact, Samantha Dunn's cleavage is so low that she explains to me if she moves her arm the wrong way her nipples will come up.

"Not unlike the sun over the Riviera," I remark casually.

I talk cocktail talk with the wives. Their husbands have gone to the toilets, to the bars, to the food stations, all networking, shaking hands, saying something witty. In Hollywood you don't give people your business card; if you are truly cool you give them preprinted cards with your cell-phone number.

A lot of money has been spent on this party; hundreds of thousands of dollars worth of food, liquor, and

eight-foot-high bouquets of fresh white orchids, garde-
nias and white roses.

The Shrine's ballroom has been done up by the
party-planning group CEI as Café Ta-Ba-Ris, a Buenos
Aires nightclub from the late Forties. There are sixteen
tango dancers, a fourteen-piece band, enormous buffets
of Argentinean food, every cocktail on earth and a lot
of beautiful faces, male and female. You can cut the
avarice in the air with a knife.

Samantha spots Alan Parker and is off into the crowd,
breasts heaving and tape recorder in hand. The men
have still left their wives alone.

These "suits" suddenly remind me of small boys in a
sandbox, or at the beach, with their plastic pails and
scoopers, all of them ready to build a sandcastle, the
biggest sandcastle of all time. They have been laughing,
kicking over towers and turrets, and they begin building again.

The wives are tapping their nails on the white linen
tablecloth. Some apply makeup, a never-ending task
when perfection is the rule. Some apply perfume, tiny
bottles hidden in their Judith Liebers, sparkling metal
bags that resemble butterflies, frogs and eggs.

"Oh look, there's Melanie Griffith and Antonio Banderas," I say excitedly. All heads turn as the couple,
with two of Melanie's children by various husbands,
walk slowly by our table. There is an audible sigh
among the women over Antonio Banderas, who is
probably one of the most beautiful men who has ever
lived, and he looks intense, sexy, but not available.
Melanie Griffith, dressed in a low-cut black number
with *lots* of straps in the back, is almost a platinum

blonde, with tight curls and red lips. The two are real honest-to-God movie stars. I cannot look away.

Melanie has a wonderfully snotty smile on her face, which I realize says to every woman in the ballroom, "I have the most gorgeous man alive. And what have *you* been doing with *your* life lately?"

"I hate her. I desperately hate her," says wife number one, in a black velvet, spaghetti strap dress. She snaps her Judith Lieber bag shut and takes two pills from a prescription bottle, then swallows them down with the end of a double vodka martini.

"Don't forget to eat the olive," I say archly. Wife number one stares blankly at me. Obviously the pills haven't kicked in.

"She's fat. Did you see her hips?" asks wife number two, in a pale beige sequined dress, a very Marilyn Singing "Happy Birthday" to John Kennedy kind of dress.

"She's a tramp. I hate her," says wife number three, who hasn't taken off her ranch mink coat all night, and the ballroom is extremely warm.

"Why her?" asks wife number four, a big, slightly drunk redhead in layers of dark burgundy chiffon. She leans in closer. "What makes *her* so special?"

"I can take a couple of guesses," I say sweetly.

"She doesn't deserve him. I hate-hate-hate her," says wife number one, her speech slowing down considerably.

To change the subject I mention the PETA demonstrators outside, decrying the use of real fur in *Evita*.

"Screw them," says wife number three, sinking further into her ranch mink coat.

"Alec Baldwin and Kim Basinger are very serious about the use of fur," I remark, "and they've come out publicly against it."

"Screw all of them," says wife number three.

"Honey, Alec Baldwin *is* a fur coat," says wife number four.

"I think his chest hair is very sexy," I say kindly. And I do, too.

Wife number two pipes up. "Sorry, but he's just too damn hairy. Men like that leave hair all over the sheets. You got to take a Hoover to them afterward. No thanks."

"I really hate Kim Basinger," mumbles wife number one, who is feeling no pain. "She doesn't deserve him."

"What is it with these bottle blondes?" asks wife number two with the rouge of skepticism.

"Well, we're in Hollywood, for one thing," I whisper, "and just look around."

Suddenly the men are back, smiling, having dealt their cards. Mountains will tumble, I think to myself, but I seriously think CAA is forever.

"Hi honey, did you see Melanie and Tony?" asks wife number two to her husband, who nods his head.

"They're just *great people,* you know?" says husband number two.

"They're great kids. Real down to earth," says husband number four.

"Baby, we've got lunch with Melanie and Antonio at Michael's. Thursday," says husband number one to his wife, who is beginning to nod off. I realize this girl didn't take aspirin. More like industrial strength Xanax.

Yet she rallies forth. "I hate Michael's. The food stinks

and the ceilings are too low," growls wife number one before closing her eyes.

"Melanie's a great talent," says husband number three to the entire table. "They're nice kids."

"They're gorgeous," I say with determination.

Husband number three looks me over carefully. "Who the hell are you?"

"I'm a writer."

"Oh Christ. Who in *hell* sat a *writer* at the table with us? I'm calling CEI in the morning."

"I'm not interested in you either," I say quietly.

After lines like that I wish I had a cigarette to light up as a calculated gesture, but I quit years ago. Joan Crawford always got enormous mileage out of her cigarettes. She'd say something *fierce,* then tap her cigarette on whatever bar she happened to be near. And sure enough, the man always lit her up.

"Christ," husband number three huffs. I decide to take a different tack.

"No, I'm a real writer. I write novels. Do you understand?" Perhaps I should hold up a drawing with stick figures and large letters.

"Sure. Sure. Books. Later."

Then he thinks for a moment and looks at me.

"You don't have one of those hidden recorders, do you?"

"No."

"Fine."

He turns away from me and talks to his cronies. The wives also turn back to their circle, and I quickly understand that I am a good, solid outsider. I will never be let in. Unless, of course, I'm their client. Then, like

Alec Baldwin, Kim Basinger, Melanie Griffith and Antonio Banderas, I'll turn into a nice kid. And a great talent.

Samantha, having gotten her interviews, returns to my table and leans over me, exposing breasts the size of small revolving planets. Conversation among the men halts immediately.

"Donald, we've got another party in Bel Air. We have to go." Again the hurried voice.

Wife number two becomes feverish.

"It's the one Madonna's going to, isn't it? I heard about it." Her eyes plead.

"Sure. Sounds great," I say.

Upon leaving the private party of the premiere of the decade, with the biggest stars in the world, I am quite tired. All this hugeness has taken its toll.

Madonna, and her immense centipede of photographers and flashbulbs, is also slowly moving toward an exit. She is tired too, I realize. Artifice of this magnitude lasts only so long, then you have to beat a retreat.

I decide tonight is just big-big-big. In this playground of spoiled children, we have all the wet sand we need, and we are just waiting for the *next big wave* to break.

Suicide in
Las Vegas

*H*ell is expensive. This is my first thought as my plane lands in Las Vegas. The Luxor Hotel's glass pyramid seems dangerously close to the runway's edge, as do its chocolate and gold sphinx and rows of shaved palms. I wonder if these rooms lightly shake when jets land. Behind the Luxor are mountains kissed by dust the hue of bone; to its left, the Strip, where color is so bright it looks like it has died, rotted and come back as a poisonous flower.

I have been forewarned. First, I am told that flying in at noon is "not the way to enter Vegas." Correct entry is at night. This way I would have the full treatment of neon and glowing sky. As a child I was taught not to buy into anything at night. The spoiled, chipped or dangerous could be easily disguised. Yet here, in the fastest-growing city in the United States, there is an appropriate "way to enter."

Exiting is not always so simple. Las Vegas has the highest suicide rate per capita in the country. This coincides with its enormous expansion, yet its suicides are dangerous myths for a city poised to become America's new economic icon. Tourists taking their lives surrounded by the glamour of the Strip are a small percentage of the fatalities. It is those who moved here for jobs, who live just beyond the lights: Ten times as many residents kill themselves here as do visitors.

Second, I am told that in Las Vegas I will feel more alive. Anything can be had here; this is the last place before the millennium where real money can be made. An open season, like America used to be. My friends in Los Angeles, who seem to know such things, say forget about winning. This is the town where you get to stub your cigarettes out in an egg, sunny side up, at four o'clock in the morning. If you can remember what time it is, and you won't, and then get in your car and drive.

This will happen before I leave. But I will be driving just to get the stink of suicide out of my chest. On Paradise Road, near a white asphalt lot with empty Boeing 707s, I will sit in my car watching early morning business flights descend into the starch of a Nevada dawn and I will suddenly see how Las Vegas is our new mirror. Into how things are going to be done. And who will win or lose.

There's a small but steady amount of suicides we call 'jumpers,' " states Sergeant Bill Keeton of Metro Police. "They're generally tourists. Some jump off an overpass, even Hoover Dam, but casinos are first choice. Balconies. The hotels wised up. Roofs stay locked."

Las Vegas has other names for its fatalities. "Snowbirds" are retirees from the Northwest who settle here or come to gamble their pension funds. "Downwinders" are Nevada residents fighting cancer who lived downwind of radioactive breezes in the Sixties. Nuclear testing was only one desert valley away; like the airport now, it was so close hotel rooms shook.

"It's not necessarily gamblers. Just people who've planned one last fling. We used to get a lot from Los Angeles. Now it's people from all over the world. We had a young man fly in from Ireland. On his immigration card it said he seemed either on drugs or depressed. He came here and went to a pistol range, shot targets for a while, then took his gun into a bathroom and killed himself. His family in Ireland kept asking, Why Las Vegas? At that same pistol range, a man from Japan shot himself in his shooting stall. It's strange."

I hear other stories. Of a wealthy man from Malibu, in the computer business, who committed suicide with sleeping pills and a plastic bag in a luxury suite at the Mirage. His body was found next to the room's baby grand piano. He had bad relations with his ex-wife. There was a suicide note, resulting in a family court battle. In Nevada, suicide notes can be interpreted as legal wills. As I listen to the story I realize it will be told again, and often, into the next century. It is part of the city now, part of its dazzle.

"You have to remember, these are the visitors. Lots of people move here and lose everything. They have to work their way out of town."

Again, a sense of lore. Las Vegas considers itself a destination, an extremely lucrative word. It is a destination summing up our desires for a decade. Like 1930s Hollywood and San Francisco in the Sixties, Las Vegas is building palaces that will not age well, and the difference, the scar under the makeup, is that people are moving here not for fame or a communal sense of idealized youth but only to survive.

Since I have been in Las Vegas I have not seen clouds. I am beginning to doubt their existence. Driving east on Las Vegas Boulevard toward Nellis Air Force Base, the sky gets bigger the poorer the road gets. I look up. It is a radiant, pure aqua.

Trailer parks are haphazardly formed on desert lots without paved roads or streetlights. Here the desert nights must shimmer. Cement-block houses without floors or windows have children running past Harley-Davidsons. I see dented Cadillacs and Lincoln Continentals from the early 1970s parked in front of tents. These cars were our grandparents' idea of elegance. Now they transport families, sleep children in the backseat, with pots and pans in the trunk; and if you can keep gas in the tank, they'll drive cross-country. I also notice that none of these cars have Nevada plates.

On the other side of town, Flamingo and Sahara Roads splay out from the Strip into the suburbs of Desert Shores, The Lakes and Spring Valley. Here "family lifestyle" communities are walled and gated and built on a massive scale. They differ slightly in both size and price from "country club lifestyle" communities like Los Prados and Deerbrook Estates, which have golf courses and ponds with bought, recirculated water. Real estate prices in 1994 are no longer a bargain. They are now comparable to Orange County or Scottsdale, Arizona. I reason the most original thing Nevada has ever had is

Las Vegas Boulevard. Respectability could mean a small death to Las Vegas.

"Not so," argues Mark Moreno, a lawyer and longtime Las Vegas resident. "The position of Las Vegas as a family entertainment destination is best for gaming right now. There are three men responsible for the new Las Vegas. Bill Bennett at Circus Circus, Kirk Kekorian with the MGM Grand, and Steve Wynn with the Mirage."

I imagine asking these three wise kings about the suicides in their hotels. The suicides of their employees in tract apartments and trailer parks facing desert mountains. The MGM Grand employs over seven thousand people on any given day. Circus Circus owns the Luxor. Circus Circus is where I try my first slot machine. The casino is a silvery pink outside, like foil wrapping for cheap candy. It is a color children will remember, and they run through its gardens and circus exhibits and play centers. Their parents gamble in the main casino. And I wonder who is responsible for the flip side of myth.

Something's missing here. I don't know how to describe it. But something's wrong."

In a Chinese restaurant on Flamingo, Allison, a stout young woman wearing eyeliner to make her eyes look Asian, shuffles her weight from one leg to the other in front of my table.

"What's missing?" I ask.

"I don't know. I have two boys, one girl. We moved here for a fresh start, me and the kids. No man at all. Everything's cool. We got a nice condo we rent at Rock

Springs Vista. I tried for the Grand but it was already filled up, so I work here. We like Lake Mead. And snow in the mountains. But the kids want to move on. So do I."

"Why?" My voice is low. Confiding. Allison walks over to an air-conditioning unit hidden behind a carved gold panel and turns it up higher so we can both only hear air. She begins to whisper.

"I just want to get the hell out of Las Vegas. Anywhere." She pauses to pour my lukewarm jasmine tea. "Here you hate the word 'money.' I can't save any money. The city eats it up. Somehow, every quarter and nickel. I work steady and where does it go?"

It is over eighty-five degrees on the third day of March. The coroner's office is located in a dusty white cement-block building with candy-apple-red trim. Inside, the friendly staff files everything there is to know about murder, suicide and death in Clark County, Nevada. Coroner Ron Flud's office is filled with trophies, plants and photographs, not unlike a career counselor's at a small-town college. Flud clasps his hands, studying me, and begins.

"First, gambling suicides in Las Vegas are minimal. It's one or two every ten years. Residents form the highest core group. And it's almost always from alienation in a relationship. Or career. Las Vegas is not always what they imagined."

I think of Allison, working her way out of town. She is not alone. As a young man, serial killer John Wayne Gacy worked his way out of Las Vegas by being a pallbearer at over seventy-five funerals at a local mortuary. In his last interview, Gacy remarked that being in prison was like "being in Las Vegas, where you're gambling and you don't know what's going on outside."

I realize everyone even remotely connected to suicide here takes great pains to assure me it does not happen from gambling. One does not kill the golden calf in Clark County.

It is axiomatic that relationships disintegrate due to money problems. In Las Vegas and its suburbs, one primary cause for personal financial stress is gambling. Its influence is a perennial one, a perfume in full bloom. There are slot machines softly crying for new parents in supermarkets in Green Valley and Henderson, in gas stations right off the freeway. It is easy to cash a paycheck at a "locals" casino like the Silver Nugget, and get free drink tickets. This does not happen in a bank.

Even the language, somewhere between cowboy and psychopath, has an optimistic inflection, still entirely Old West, that here you can get something for nothing. This has always been a lie. People are moving to Las Vegas at the rate of six thousand per month. They hear the words "no taxes, jobs, good weather." They have come to make money for a year, then leave. Many wind up unable to make the rent.

"There's a sense of anonymity and transience here," notes Flud. "If someone dies and we have an address over two years old we'll have to question its accuracy. That's how often Las Vegans move."

Statistics show the most popular form of self-inflicted death in Las Vegas is by gunshot, using a handgun. Second is by hanging, third is by lethal ingestion of drugs, often mixed with alcohol. In Ron's office, I see how creative desperation can be. Every year includes deaths by carbon-monoxide inhalation, cutting wounds, jumping from heights, stabbing self, electrocution, a plastic bag over the head, asphyxia from charcoal fire, self-immolation with gasoline, deliberate car wrecks, cyanide and industrial poisons, self-set residential fires, decapitation by train, even lethal amounts of dirt and grass forced into the mouth (achieved in a 1990 Las Vegas suicide).

"Being a gaming town, there's a lot of Russian roulette. It's a mistake to think it's a game. It's a very successful form of suicide."

This simple connection chills my arms. I think of a gun being passed around. A trigger being pulled. Laughter. Deliberate prayers whispered as sprinklers water brown desert lawns. I think how, downtown on Fremont, where white neon lights never stop, there is no music. I expect Dixieland jazz, saxophones, trumpets, but there is only silence. Elderly casino patrons shuffle past snowbirds and downwinders on their way to Binion's Horseshoe and the Lady Luck. Many come to lose one hundred dollars—that's the budget—and many will not live to return. And in that silence, someone in the city is lifting a loaded gun, emptying a prescription, or eating dirt until their heart convulses.

Big suicide months are December and January. The largest suicide group is those between the ages of thirty and thirty-nine. After the age of fifty, numbers drop significantly. Three times as many men kill themselves as do women. Most statistics do not change from city to city. Systematic and severe depression are not born solely in Las Vegas. The difference here is the postcard in the background. Neon lights. The smell of money. And the sense of a soul's exhaustion, ready to pass through those neon lights.

I realize Las Vegas is a silent city because all the action is inside. When we kill ourselves our plans succeed because they are secret. As a vindictive act, suicide's damage is permanent. And the question of *why* cannot be answered by anyone alive.

"*Why* is the word," Flud stresses quietly. "Why would a man and woman from Southern California drive across the state line into Nevada, park just over the border and shoot themselves to death in the front seat of their car? Why would a man in bed with a woman in a hotel on Fremont say something like 'I'm going to teach you a lesson' and then blow his brains out on top of her? This woman wound up severely traumatized. Why would someone do this?"

Because they're working their way out of town, I think to myself. Because something is missing. In the late Eighties a young man shot himself to death at Lake Mead. He had a tattoo of a heart on his chest, and that's where he pointed the gun. Underneath the tattoo was a date, freshly inked, on his skin. When his ex-wife called the coroner to find out the details of his death, she gasped. The date under his heart, shy of a close-range bullet wound, was the day, month and year their divorce became final.

Sometimes they are criminal, attracted to the glamour of not going back. Judge John C. Fairbanks, seventy, of New Hampshire, stole $1.8 million from his private law practice clientele, disappeared the day he was indicted—on December 28, 1989—and hid out for years. On Thursday, March 24, 1994, Fairbanks checked into the MGM Grand under an assumed name. On Sunday he was found dead.

Judge John C. Fairbanks was not a casual man. He succeeded at everything he set out to do. His suicide note, written to his son, who had already been called by Fairbanks from his residence in Canada, was taped to the mirror. This means that Fairbanks got to take a good look at himself before he went.

This is almost myth. Fairbanks's actions say to the desperate: I had the thrill of stealing millions. I had the thrill of never going back. If you're going to check out, do it in the city of instant gratification, in the biggest hotel in the world. Do it in Las Vegas.

The reality is that Judge John C. Fairbanks killed himself by using a hotel shoe bag over his head. The bag was plastic, with a drawstring, normally put outside rooms for shoes to be polished and redelivered. He used rubber bands around his neck to attach the bag securely over his head. It was off-white, and presumably he could not see either light or dark as parts of the bag slid into his mouth, toward his throat and up into his nasal cavities. Perhaps children were running down the hall outside his room as he suffocated. Perhaps their parents were arguing over lost money in the casino. Judge John C. Fairbanks died in silence. Alone.

It is 9:15 P.M. and the Congo Theatre of the Sahara Hotel is dark. Kenny Kerr is in between shows of his female impersonation revue, *Boylesque.* I am ushered into a beige dressing room. Kerr, sans wig but in flawless women's makeup, is smoking Marlboro cigarettes in a glittery caftan.

"The first rule in Las Vegas: If you work here, don't drink and don't gamble. And you have to have a sense of humor, and remember where you've come from."

I explain to Kerr about the suicide rate in Las Vegas. He taps his nails on the edge of his leather recliner and continues.

"I'm not surprised. It gets real heavy here. I've put friends through rehab for drugs and alcohol. I do it because I care. See, honey, here, if the devil isn't staring you right in the face then he's just around the corner."

Little Lil, the 350-pound comedy drag in the show, agrees with Kerr.

"I got lots of stories on the devil in Las Vegas. I helped a friend once who lost everything in a casino. House, bank account, car, the works. He was high as a kite on the Flamingo overpass, ready to jump. I got him down."

I drive to the Flamingo overpass. The lights of Las Vegas are a fuzzy blue; below, cars on the freeway sound like slot machines in the night wind. It is a sound I cannot escape, and it is twenty-four hours a day. This ramp has signs that read NO ENTRY, and I think of mirrors with bad lighting in Las Vegas hotels. They murmur you've gotten old, you're going to fail. Because you came to Las Vegas to lose.

I am sitting poolside at the Sahara Hotel with Jackie, a receptionist at Mark Moreno's office. She called me earlier with the information that her husband had shot himself to death three months ago. She tells me she writes poetry and keeps a journal. She says it keeps her alive.

The gardens surrounding the pool are sleepy and shaded. The only noise is mockingbirds hopping through olive trees. Jackie has soft red hair and green eyes. She is thirty-one years old. Jackie quietly shows me pictures of her two sons, Matt and Chris, aged ten and eight, respectively.

"David and I got married in 1981. He was a captain in the U.S. Army. We did a lot of traveling like army families do. You make your home where you hang your hat. We used to say that. Then David was affected by the military cutbacks in 1991. He was passed over for major, then the army sort of let him go. He was devastated. This happened in Pittsburg, Kansas."

Jackie lights a cigarette and puts on her sunglasses.

"We had been here on a trip and thought it was paradise. So first my mom and sister moved to Las Vegas, then I sold the house in Pittsburg and moved the boys and myself out here. David was in Germany teaching. We got an apartment at Desert Shores. The boys couldn't wait for Dad to come back. You know, David was an extremely confident man."

Jackie lowers her sunglasses and looks at me.

"I'm sure he was very confident. He was an army man," I say.

"Exactly. I got a job teaching but it wasn't much pay. When David came home he thought a job would be a piece of cake. First David had a job, working on commission, for an insurance firm. A 'sales and suit job,' he called it. It didn't work out. David came home from a military physical in 1993 with a note saying he was severely depressed. He threw it down on the kitchen counter and laughed. I didn't pay any attention. Jesus. David wound up working as a security guard, the night shift, and he hated it. Can you imagine? A captain? He had become so horribly . . . disappointed."

"You had no idea?" I ask.

"None. David killed himself on December 7. Just like that. The boys and David and I were playing UNO, a family card game, in the kitchen, before they had to go to school. It was David's day off and he had a new job interview late that afternoon, so I asked my mom, Jean, to babysit the boys. I remember David made a big point of walking me to the front door and kissing me when I left for work. Then he tried calling me at work but I couldn't talk. I was busy."

Jackie goes on to explain that they had an eviction notice delivered that day, the second in a month. David had planned his suicide for at least three months prior. Jackie remembers wearing a red dress and red shoes to work. She came home from work to be met by her mother, who was running late. The boys were at a neighbor's house. On the front door was a letter addressed to Jean, Jackie's mother. It was in David's handwriting. The first sentence read: "Dear Jean, please don't be angry with me but I have taken my life."

Jackie says there was a moment that was indescribable. As Jean continued to read the letter, Jackie became hysterical. Jean called 911. In the letter David detailed exactly where his body would be found: on a corner lot at Charleston and Apple, not two blocks from their home. And about two hundred yards in from the street. Jackie also discovered David had left her a letter, a letter to each of their sons and a videotape.

"David shot himself through the head with a pistol, military style, pointing the gun up, at an angle beneath his right ear. He knew what he was doing. It was a neat, clean shot. We were able to show the body at the reception."

Jackie's voice begins to crack. She lights another cigarette. I notice she has two wedding rings, her own and David's, molded together on a gold chain around her neck.

"With his left hand he was holding a picture of the boys, and a picture of him and me in dressy clothes. I was in a white dress. We were going to renew our vows in a wedding chapel on the Strip in February 1994. . . . He killed himself at sunset, facing Red Rock Canyon. He loved Red Rock."

Jackie remembers running from the apartment those two blocks, seeing the police helicopter with its searchlights, seeing her husband's body bag put into the coroner's wagon, and thinking, This has got to be some kind of joke. She remembers screaming at a policewoman who made a disparaging remark, and that her mother had to hold her back.

"Then I had to go home and tell my sons. You try telling two young boys their father has just shot himself through the head. You damn well try that on for size."

Jackie began to cry. She buries her head in her hands. I excuse myself, telling her I need to use the restroom, and she nods her head knowingly. Inside the men's room at the Sahara Hotel, halfway between a pool and a casino, with a beaten, victimized woman outside, I turn toward the mirror to connect, however briefly, with myself, but the mirrors have been removed. I begin to shake and hold on to the sink. I don't cry. There is no point.

It is dusk. Jackie lights one more cigarette as I sit down. Her eyes are dry, focusing on the now lit pool.

"It's pretty here," she says quietly. The Sahara sign begins its blue and white blink. All the false moons are lighting the sky over Las Vegas.

"I'll tell you who I blame. I blame the U.S. Army for turning men into officers. That's who I blame. And Las Vegas. What a joke. Why must everything in life wind down to a joke?" She shakes her head. "I'm moving the boys and me to Pittsburg in May."

This conversation takes place on the fourth of March, 1994. Thursday evening. Tonight, my last night in Las Vegas, I will not be able to sleep, and at four o'clock in the morning I will begin to drive.

In Los Angeles several months later, I call Jackie's apartment. A man answers the phone. I sound bewildered. Jackie, he states, is getting the boys ready and packed, the apartment cleaned out, she's still working at the law office, she's busy. When I ask this man who he is, he laughs.

"Who, me? Friend, I'm the new husband."

Jackie waves to me as she pulls her car onto Las Vegas Boulevard. The slot machines inside the Sahara's casino are chattering like drugged children. I feel unclean, as though I have been bitten by something contagious that hides in the dark. At the casino's doors I turn and look at the city beyond, silent, crawling with a low, sexual glitter. It burns a blue not unlike a gas cooking flame turned down, barely touching its own air, until it is only a hiss.

This Las Vegas blue is the Stardust Hotel lit each evening, the Sahara sign going toward the bad end of the Strip. It is the blue of the darkened Congo Theatre before Kenny Kerr performs, and the blue leftovers of sunsets that attend suicides. It is how poverty creates its own blue skies, hoping God will be kind in a town leaving nothing to chance. It is the whispered question before the trigger is pulled, the last blue moment when all we can ask is *Why*.

WOLFGANG PETERSEN

Almost nothing in Hollywood is a sure bet. And if someone tells you you're looking at a sure bet, don't work with them because in the end, somehow you'll get screwed. Like the words "Trust me."

Yet corporate tactics insist there must be a method, some science to predict box office. Public taste changes. So advertise with a new look. Same products, new look. Use more special effects. Throw money at a problem and it will go away.

This is often achieved at the expense of the original story. An easy complaint is that the studios can never find a good story. In this arena filmmakers have a long career if they instinctively know a good story and can translate it into a commercial picture. Art films and small dramas don't count and are basically throw-the-dog-a-bone items. I am speaking of the high end of Hollywood: studio projects expected to gross over—hopefully way over—$100 million. Domestically.

Filmmaker Wolfgang Petersen is one of the few sure bets working within the studio system. He has become, over the past eight years, a quintessential Hollywood director in the mold of W. S. Van Dyke, who directed *The Thin Man* series; or John Ford, the legendary, and cantankerous, creator of over seventy classic films. In a sense, Petersen is old fashioned in that he creates solid entertainment in different genres that make enormous profit. This is what studios like.

Many of Petersen's Hollywood films will be considered classics in the next twenty years, as John Ford's films are today. His *Das Boot* is a classic already. Petersen's touch can always be seen in a tight script, the production gloss of studio money and big stars.

Wolfgang Petersen's office is on the second floor at Tri-Star and it is a quiet place, simple and without grandeur. I expected designer furniture, a suite of Picasso etchings hung perfectly across a wall. I remind myself the only people in Hollywood who have those kind of offices are talent agents, and that is a pretension that goes with the territory.

Petersen is a good-looking German man with gray-blue eyes and wispy, longish blond hair. He is very direct, with an evenly modulated voice. It is a voice of tremendous patience. His demeanor is that of an artist, but without the affectations.

"I arrived in America, from Germany, in 1987, with my wife, Maria, and four suitcases. We had come to Hollywood to do a film with Kathleen Turner called *Alicia's Book,* which fell apart. That was my first lesson. Projects fall apart all the time."

Petersen pauses, studying me, then continues.

"I don't think you will ever understand what it was like in Germany after the war. I grew up in Emden, in the north of Germany; at that time everything was ravaged. I remember as a little boy running to see American ships and they tossed food to us. It was the first time I'd seen a banana, or an orange. I admired Gary

Cooper, the movie star. I wanted, by the age of ten, to direct movies. So you see, I did not come to Hollywood as a stranger."

Petersen quietly recounts that after finishing film school in 1970, he made over twenty-five films as a director; two-hour movies for German television.

"That was an exciting time. There were only two channels in Germany, and I worked constantly, guaranteed a viewership of most of Germany. Then, of course, came *Das Boot.*"

As his career propelled forward in the Eighties, the next logical step was Hollywood, and Hollywood, for the last fifty to seventy years, has had an affinity for German directors. Consider Fritz Lang, Ernst Lubitsch, Josef von Sternberg, Erich von Stroheim, Max Reinhardt. And, of course, Billy Wilder.

"Today you have to be more than a director; you have to be a good businessman, organized, a producer, a top manager, psychiatrist, accountant, money man. It used to be a film crew for a major picture was twenty-five people. Now it's over two hundred people."

We discuss power and what it means in Hollywood. I mention how agents and producers are as important as the studios themselves. Petersen grins.

"Yes and no. It is still a star-driven business. More than ever. If a famous actor and a director can agree on a picture, then that's a picture that'll get made. All it takes is a Clint Eastwood or a Stallone to say yes. Or for a Sharon Stone or a Demi Moore to say yes."

Petersen discusses how stars sell movies. Now they are full-time commodities whose image sells product. "That's why Demi Moore can ask $12.5 million for her next picture," I interject. "Or Jim Carrey's new $20 million price tag."

"The international market is huge," Petersen continues, "and there are more ways than ever to make money. A big studio film today plays all over the world, then video all over the world, then television rights, film libraries."

I bemoan a certain lack of glamour, thinking of how stars of the Thirties and Forties seemed like real stars, other-worldly beings, and now they don't seem like anyone at all.

"It's the times we live in. But that does not mean that great movies cannot be made. They are being made all the time."

Petersen's recent films, such as *In the Line of Fire* with Clint Eastwood, *Shattered* with Tom Berenger and *Outbreak* with Dustin Hoffman, have tight plots and deal with current issues. They also have a fair amount of violence. Recently there has been a huge backlash, by presidential candidate Bob Dole and various conservative political groups, against excessively violent entertainment.

"Violence cannot be ignored in the Nineties," Petersen stresses in his patient voice. I worry I hit a nerve. He continues.

"But where is the limit? Where do you go from using it as part of a great, entertaining story, like *Shattered* or *In the Line of Fire,* to exploiting violence just to get more people into the theater? And the subsequent, possible damage. For me, personally, I don't like to deal with excessive violence. There are a lot more interesting ways to entertain an audience." I nod my head.

"If you're like myself, with three or four great new stories, and the financing to make them into films, then you're in heaven. I love movies. That's why I'm here. I love Santa Monica, my wife, my house, my pets. I'm a very happy man. We don't play all the Hollywood social games. I enjoy being German."

"Generally, the Hollywood games are played by people who are trying to get work, not by those people who are working," I comment.

The Mexican wind has started up and I can see palm trees rustling. The sun is suddenly very clear and hot. I ask Petersen if he feels he has fulfilled his dreams.

"Yes," he counters without hesitation. "I'm in Hollywood, making movies. I've worked hard and I've been lucky. The movie business is becoming increasingly complex, though. I think a dream situation would be one film every year and a half, with a four-month prep; maybe produce movies every year and a half. But that, you know, is just a dream."

THE ISOTTA FRASCHINI

Particular memories stand out, not because of what happened but what didn't; often they say more about myself than I am willing to admit. I remember a car, this long, elegant, ridiculous car, and I remember I felt I belonged to it, and that, somehow, it belonged to me.

It was a clear, sunny day, almost hot. I was driving a sea-mist green 1969 Cadillac down the western, residential section of Hollywood Boulevard, in 1980. Or near 1980; perhaps it was the autumn of 1979. Regardless, it was a happy day. I was twenty-three, working as a film extra and thoroughly enjoying my blossoming sexual appetite.

I loved my Cadillac; its sea-mist green paint I thought very glamorous and elegant. Color and make of any car is always important to note in Los Angeles. It defines the memory, as the real experiences of this city seldom happen anywhere that isn't moving. Your car is the place to be. You see it all.

I had bought my car from an elderly lady named Connie, who lived in a bungalow in Reseda with a tomato patch in her front yard. She let it go for five hundred dollars, which was all I could afford at the time. And what a deal. I drove off with a basket of fresh tomatoes from Connie in the backseat.

So, on this first day of being a Cadillac person, I let the Hollywood Boulevard air caress my long hair and listened to Earth, Wind and Fire on an FM channel. I was at the intersection of Hollywood and Fairfax, the deep foliage of the Hollywood Hills above me. Los Angeles was swept clean of dust by a Pacific breeze that reeked of seaweed and motorboat oil.

A car pulled up next to me. I was stunned, as I thought it didn't exist; a 1929 Isotta Fraschini, newly painted, with an open-air backseat and chauffeur separation. The works. The back of the car was upholstered in leopard-skin velvet; the chauffeur was wearing black leather, like Erich von Stroheim, stone-faced, of course. And wearing a monocle.

In the back, a woman was in black velvet with a white-egret feather hat, smoking a cigarette in a rhinestone holder, and fluttering her hands in a very louche manner. Her companion was dressed in a padded-shoulder cream-colored suit from the Forties, and I realized they were playing Norma Desmond and Joe Gillis. Looking closer, I also noticed the woman had the same surrealistic makeup Swanson wore in the 1950 film *Sunset Boulevard,* the same way of baring her teeth like a hyena, and I assumed this was all for fun, a realization of one more Hollywood dream, close to twelve years before Andrew Lloyd Webber was to "re-discover" Norma and Joe. But what I adored was that this Norma Desmond was very much a man, in full and exceptionally careful drag.

In Hollywood I have seen real-life Baby Jane Hudsons wandering through drugstores in Glendale, eighty years old with pigtails, gingham dress and white, powdered face. I have been out for drunken dinners with Marilyn Monroe lookalikes who last a year here, then move back to the quieter parts of Wisconsin. I understand the grotesque beauty of failure, and here it is an art form, even in the Nineties, when we pride ourselves at being beyond illusion.

But nothing that day had prepared me for the Isotta Fraschini; the chauffeur revved the engine several times, and this afternoon vision of Norma Desmond popped a peppermint in her mouth and, with a smile made out of concrete, turned to glance at me. The wind blew the egret feathers on her hat. I was being assimilated, decided upon, tossed aside. You see, I was a fan, staring at the gods at a stoplight. With his mouth open.

Camp, in all of Susan Sontag's various dissertations, certainly comes to mind, but at that moment gender made no difference. The point being that I lived in Hollywood. I got the joke. I understood. This does not happen in Ohio.

I often wonder who the group was; whether they worked at a studio, a hair salon, a hamburger stand, an auto-repair shop. Someone spent some money for this afternoon lark.

Now, on a recent trip into West Hollywood for their annual Halloween riots, I saw a 1962 Lincoln Continental touring convertible, with suicide doors, Secret Service men, little American flags and Jackie Kennedy in drag, same suit, pink and sweet, and the pillbox hat. Next to her was a handsome man, another exact replica of John F. Kennedy. I shuddered. I was later told that at some point during the evening, Mr. Kennedy would pretend to be shot, and Mrs. Kennedy would dump a bowl of SpaghettiOs all over the front of her pink Chanel suit, then crawl over the back of the Lincoln as it slowly made its way down Santa Monica Boulevard, to laughter and flashbulbs.

We are an ugly bunch, those of us who are surviving the millennium. I prefer to remember when I was young and beautiful, idling next to Norma Desmond in an Isotta Fraschini. How the light turned green, and she continued to smile at me with immense, gritted teeth, then imperiously waved her chauffeur to drive on.

Our lady
OF THE LIONS

I once had my picture taken with an old lioness at a swap meet in Alachua, Florida. She was sprawled on an Oriental rug in the center of a small tent. Chained and drugged, there were sores on her hind and around her eyes. Flies clustered on her mouth. Ten feet away was a camera and an overweight biker. For five dollars, I sat on a pillow next to the big cat; before the camera clicked, the biker pulled up her head so it looked like she was conscious, then walked away. It is something I remember, and regret.

When I tell Tippi Hedren this story, she studies me with a smooth, emotionless face, then asks me if I am positive the lioness was drugged. I say yes. She nods her head, allowing me my sincerity, then walks over to a Bengal tiger named Dagger, who has been waiting for her. Dagger is pacing back and forth behind his chain-link fence. Tippi gives him a big kiss on the nose, coos a bit and scratches his head. She then turns to me, looking into my eyes.

"These are my friends."

It is the middle of August, and I am at Shambala, Hedren's home in Soledad Canyon. Here she lives with nineteen lions, four African servals, six cougars, nine leopards including a rare Himalayan snow leopard, a cheetah, black panthers, nine tigers, an iguana, a python, boa constrictors, a Vietnamese pot-bellied pig, house cats, two African elephants, several thousand red-winged blackbirds, mallard ducks, coots, cockatoos and toucans.

In this canyon of salmon-colored rock, Tippi Hedren has created her own sovereignty, a rarefied and exotic world thirty minutes from Encino. Shambala, in Sanskrit, means "a meeting place of peace and harmony for all beings, animal and human." On over sixty acres, Shambala is dreamlike, bordering on fantasy; an inherent characteristic of Southern California. If you have the land, you can follow your heart. And the world outside stays that way.

Shambala began as a movie set for a film Hedren and ex-husband Noel Marshall made called *Roar,* most of whose cast was populated by big cats. It still stands, like the old backlot at Twentieth Century Fox, in isolated and cognizant splendor. The largest set, the African House, sits quietly on its own lagoon; a ramshackle, Tennessee Williams kind of building, it looks haunted, enchanted, ready to collapse.

Inside the African House is a room full of boa constrictors and pythons, including an albino boa constrictor with creamy white scales. Another room serves as storage for Shambala T-shirts, postcards and several bolts of leopard-skin chiffon. Across the lagoon, Timbo and Kura, Hedren's two elephants, are swaying gently together in the sun; farther on, a leopard is clawing a tree the way a house cat might claw a sofa. Several lions are sprawled in the sun, on top of an ancient, windowless bus. Reeds rustle in a light summer wind.

Tippi Hedren's modest ranch house is cluttered with souvenirs from African safaris, movie memorabilia and photographs of her family. In her office, I stand next to the sliding-glass doors. A three-year-old cougar named Daisy runs toward me and stops. I brace myself against a desk. She then paws gently at the sliding-glass doors, signaling she wants to be let in, and I shake my head no.

"Oh, that's my Daisy. She wants in," says Hedren. "Isn't she a beauty?"

"Adorable," I answer.

In a fenced area of Hedren's backyard, she introduces me to her African serval, an ocelotlike cat weighing around fifty pounds with large pointed ears. Her name is Arielle. Arielle is not particularly social. I am then introduced to Subira, her pet cheetah.

"She's physically disadvantaged," Hedren says to me in a serious, no-jokes voice.

When I see Subira I pause. She is a three-legged cheetah whose left back leg was lost at birth, having been cut off by the umbilical cord. Subira walks up to me and licks my hand. Her tongue is like a rasp.

"Subira ran all the way to African House, all by herself without falling," Hedren says proudly.

This is what Tippi Hedren is about. No private owner or zoo would want Subira. In the wild she would be dead. But at Shambala she is loved, cherished. I sit next to the cheetah and she begins to purr.

"Cheetahs purr. Not all the big cats do, though. Only cheetahs, lynx, cougars and domestic cats purr," notes

Hedren. "They have a bony structure called the hyoid at the base of the tongue that creates this sound."

"It's the loudest purr I've heard," I say. Subira drapes herself over Hedren's lap and looks up at her mistress. There is a connection, a simple silence between the two, that I realize I will never attain, no matter how much affection I would give an animal. With Tippi Hedren, her understanding of big cats goes beyond what we choose to understand or verify.

"Here the wild ones only know love. Period."

Tippi Hedren is a slender, small-boned woman who would scowl if she were called petite. Like her lionesses, she emanates a shrewd control of physical gestures that has nothing to do with acting but everything to do with reflex and reaction. Like Elizabeth Taylor's, Hedren's voice is oddly pinched and childlike, yet smoky. It is a sexy voice, but one that could become quite acid if provoked.

In the animal compounds, many of the lions stand to attention and pace when Tippi Hedren walks by. She is definitely queen of the lot. She calls each animal by name, as every animal at Shambala has one, as well as a history. Suddenly the beast is humanized. In circuses and zoos we are not allowed to see past a certain psychological barrier. We become voyeurs. One lion is all lions. All tigers jump through hoops, bare their teeth, snarl.

"Big cats do not look alike. In male lions, for example, every face is different," explains Hedren. "There are subtle variances: a larger nose, cranium, mane, eyes. Each animal is unique."

I am introduced to Rowdy, a small lion taking a sunbath, who pays no attention to me. Rowdy belonged to a drug dealer and was often beaten. The tigers, Dagger and Whitey, are part of a litter of four Hedren found being sold out of a car at the Fashion Island parking lot in Newport Beach. A black panther named Kara was found abandoned in a garage in Wyoming with frostbitten paws, intestinal damage, and four inches cut off her tail. Leo the lion was found living in a basement in Branson, Missouri, and terrified of human contact; another lion, Mikey, was abandoned in a house in Yonkers, New York. Her elephant, Kura, was hit so hard in the circus she's blind in one eye.

"These animals make terrible pets," she explains, "and people forget that an adorable tiger cub grows very quickly and the owners have no idea how to cope with a big cat. Private owners will declaw them, have their canines removed. None of this is good."

We pause to feed an iguana in a large wire cage.

"Hold the door," Hedren says, "this one's mean. We are currently not friends."

The iguana hisses at Tippi, slapping its tail against the sides of its cage. Tippi pours some food into a metal bowl, dusts her denim shirt off and locks the door back up.

"There are certain things you must understand. Big cats raised in captivity still have the nature of the wild. They can be very loving, then destructive. And they will strike for no apparent reason. They can easily kill whatever is in front of them, including us, and go right back to what they were doing as if nothing happened. They have no guilt as we know it. If they see a physical change in someone, a weakness, they will go on alert; this could be food. It's instinct."

"I notice children under eighteen aren't allowed at Shambala," I say, quietly.

"It's because the female lionesses, in particular, look at anything under a certain size as food. It's serious. They become quite agitated. Have you ever seen two female cats fight? Not a pretty sight."

We walk past a black panther named Pepper, whom Tippi speaks to in a soft, knowing tone. She explains to me that Pepper is now quite old, almost twenty-one. Shade dapples the panther's sleek dark fur.

"I make this walk every day. To say hello to my friends. It's good exercise."

I think of Saint Blaise, who protects us from the wild beast, and Saint Francis, who protects all animals, probably from us. And how we are attracted to the big cats without understanding why. It is sexual, seeing ourselves in a hunter's face with curved yellow eyes. It makes us feel powerful, this perfume of blood and instinct. But we do not get too close. We are not that strong.

Remember, big cats don't deceive. They aren't like people," says Los Angeles poet Michael Gregg Michaud, who is on the board of directors of Shambala's Roar Foundation. "If they are hungry, they'll let you know. If they are angry, their body language will show it."

Michaud is a soft-spoken man who walks slowly and mulls his words.

"I became involved with Tippi and the animals five years ago. I was just fascinated by the big cats, as many are. This is an unusual facility in that it studies nonperforming animals in captivity. All training here uses affection. We're the ones learning from them."

We are standing in a gully with dense trees and vines. Near us a Himalayan snow leopard is asleep in his house, near an electric humidifier. Winston, Hedren's pot-bellied pig, comes over and nudges my knee, then trots away.

"People are cruel without realizing it," notes Michaud. "You have to *kill* an elephant to get the tusk. For a fur coat, say a serval coat, you have to kill sixty cats. For a leopard coat, six leopards or more. In the old MGM Grand in Las Vegas, they used to keep a male lion drugged and chained to a pedestal. The insignia of MGM was on the pedestal, and this was supposed to be Leo the Lion. For tourist photographs." He shakes his head in disgust.

Tippi Hedren is beyond us, on the slope of a hill covered in tall grass, visiting several lions and cougars. She turns to us and waves. Michaud looks up at the sky, then turns to me.

"Big cats have a dignity that intensifies in adverse conditions. As humans, we're envious. It's a regal quality, a grandeur we aspire to and seldom reach."

I nod my head. I always believed in movie stars, and kings and queens, as a child. That someone was meant to wear a crown. Often I still search for a sense of grandeur, even magic, and find we have trampled it over. I still believe that elephants never forget, and the lion is king of the jungle.

By 1994 we have destroyed most of these cats; the Florida panther is on the endangered-species list, the ocelot is nearly extinct. There are less than 350 Siberian tigers left in the wild. The Javanese tiger became extinct in the middle 1980s. Farm expansion deposed the Texas jaguarundi; the last known cat of this breed was run over on a Texas highway in 1986. Noblesse oblige is dead.

Tippi Hedren met her first lion in 1969, on the set of *Satan's Harvest,* filmed in Zimbabwe, Africa. His name was Dandylion. She remembers being stunned by his arrogance and regal disdain, and by how gentle he was with humans he liked. An idea was formed with Noel Marshall to make a movie with lions but to film it in Southern California. A lot of lions.

Her daughter, the actress Melanie Griffith, was then twelve years old. Going through the big cat networks, they began accumulating lions, who lived in their house on Knob Hill Drive in Sherman Oaks. As the collection of fully grown lions and cubs grew, Hedren told neighbors all the roaring was "a couple of motorcycles being revved up."

The Marshalls were good friends with William Peter Blatty, and Noel Marshall became executive producer on *The Exorcist.* Its success, along with funding from EMI and a Tokyo producer, Banjiro Uemura, help set up Shambala, originally bought as river-bottom, desert canyon land with hardly any trees. Sets, like the African

House, were built to resemble buildings in Mozambique.

The resulting film, *Roar,* was plagued by a severe flood on February 9, 1978. The entire compound was nearly destroyed; two female lionesses, Mary and Melanie, were swept downstream and subsequently shot to death by sheriff's deputies. Film was scattered for miles by the floodwaters.

Fire has been a persistent threat, particularly in August and September. Trainers and handlers have to exercise enormous skill moving agitated big cats to safer ground. Hedren feels so many of the people who work with the animals at Shambala are more psychic companions than just trainers.

Like any world unto itself, Hedren and Shambala have seen friends come and go. Death and divorce have weaved their musk into the landscape; Hedren has also become a grandmother. There is a very clean Cadillac parked in the soft dirt next to her house. Concessions are made to civilization.

When I ask her if she has ever thought of selling Shambala, if it is ever too much, she stops smiling.

"Never. I'm in this for life."

Over her years at Shambala, Tippi Hedren has had a breast nipped by a lion cub, been charged at, knocked down, scratched, bitten and clawed. A tigress named Cherries took most of Hedren's head in her mouth and bit down into her scalp and skull. In the tussle, several of Hedren's fingernails were ripped off. She remembers her face and hair covered in blood and the sound of teeth scraping bone.

The big cats eat over three tons of meat per year;

most of the cats are hand fed by feeders and sometimes by Hedren herself. When a big cat dies, Hedren takes it hard.

I learn from Hedren that lions are more social, tigers more solitary. The female has the more active brain; she's the hunter who brings home the food. When she seduces the male she flips her tail tuft under his nose or rolls on her back, sometimes sliding under him in a tease. When he responds, he is spat upon, hit, and threatened right up to the act, which takes only seconds and is repeated up to twelve times a day.

A lioness will also reject, or try to kill, a cub if she feels it is imperfect. This happened to a male cub named Billy, whom Hedren raised herself. As an adult lion, Billy became so attached to her she could not appear in front of Billy with another human. Billy would try to kill the other person. Hedren also lavished love on a "tiglon" named Noelle, whose father was a tiger and mother a lioness.

"When you live with the lions, you become impatient with much of the idiocy in human life. Sometimes I wonder if people actually can hear themselves when they speak," says Hedren.

Facing the African House is a grassy knoll with picnic tables and lawn chairs. Coots and mallard ducks scatter across the water. Beyond the knoll are the compounds of more lions, cougars, tigers. As I sit with Tippi in the shade, I realize nothing here is abandoned. Not the old sets, or the sunbathing lions, or the elephants across the lake. For the big cats of Shambala, once you are brought here, you are never lost again.

"Shambala is a sanctuary, but it is also home," notes Hedren. "We don't professionally breed animals, nor do we raise animals to sell. When they come here, this is their home for the rest of their lives. Most big cats would live six or seven years in the wild; here their life span is over twenty years."

Out of a group of reeds bordering the lake, several hundred red-winged blackbirds flutter up to the afternoon sun.

"Thousands of them live in those reeds. And the trees are cottonwoods. I've planted over eight hundred trees. Lions love them. They hug them, claw them, become quite possessive of individual trees. It's the sap."

I hear a lion roar. It startles me. Tippi laughs.

"That's the lion's roar. Now when one roars, figure more will follow."

Soon Shambala is full of the sound of roaring lions. Hedren runs her hand through her hair and crosses her legs. I remind myself that I am sitting with a film star, the last icy Hitchcock blonde. For many years Tippi Hedren did not speak of the ugliness that occurred between her and Hitchcock. Now she studies her lake and sighs.

"People think that after *The Birds* and *Marnie* that I stopped working, that Alfred Hitchcock really did ruin my career, as he said he would. That's nonsense. I continued to make pictures ever since. And television. Right now I'm working on *Dream On.*"

Before visiting Shambala, I watched *The Birds* and *Marnie*. Tippi Hedren was astonishingly beautiful and given the kind of full star treatment that no longer exists: Gowns by Edith Head. Hair by Alexandre of Paris. Loving, softened shots in close-up, her blond hair glistening. Hitchcock was smart: He placed her around animals. Tippi Hedren looks good next to an animal, something most people do not.

But it is not 1964 anymore. A shock of white runs through Tippi Hedren's blond hair; her face has very few lines, and her eyes are smart and serious. There is no pout, no icy glamour here. That mantle has been passed on to others. Now it is the lions, as it always has been. And reality.

"It's a never-ending search for funds to keep Shambala going. It can be very tiring, I'll say that. And frustrating. Right now it's running over $250,000 a year. That's food and basics. The state of California has always been very supportive, and the people of Acton . . ."

Tippi's voice trails.

"What you need is a David Geffen. Or a Barry Diller. They certainly know the language," I remark.

Hedren's eyes brighten. "Do you know them?" she asks.

"No," I answer.

Tippi Hedren curls up in a fire-engine-red Adirondack chair in the late afternoon light. She stares at her elephants, her lake of ducks, her lions and flowers, then remarks in a stage whisper: "You know, I felt like a really big spender. I bought twenty dollars worth of Lotto tickets. It's at twenty million! Could you imagine what could be done here with that kind of loot! I don't have that. I've never been particularly rich."

"I think you are," I say.

"Really?" Tippi Hedren asks. I nod my head, knowing a certain royalty is here.

Another hot breeze begins to shimmer the leaves of the cottonwoods, and the lions begin to roar.

FADE OUT

Ennis Cosby is dead, and the L.A.P.D. feels it knows who did it. "We have a lead," says a homicide detective on KABC-TV. "This murder must be priority one," states the mayor of Los Angeles, Richard Riordan.

Larry Austin, the elderly proprietor of the Silent Movie Theater in Los Angeles, is also dead. The L.A.P.D. does not know who did it. An eyewitness drawing of the killer appears this morning in the *Los Angeles Times*. Please help us find this man. What the L.A.P.D. doesn't realize is that all of Larry Austin's friends know who did it. And they're not talking.

January in Los Angeles in 1997 reeks with the perfume of madness, with crimes happening so quickly I can only catch my breath. This is the way people behave before a quake, shooting each other, driving off cliffs, screaming at the slight things in life. These January crimes are Hollywood crimes, acts of viciousness under the palms.

As of yet, I am still writing a mystery, a murder that took place in Hollywood one week ago. It is entirely probable that the L.A.P.D. will close this case in five to ten days. Maybe sooner. Why? Because the truth is all over town. It is in the whispered phone calls, the innuendo of a glance, a quiet horror that happens only here.

I remember an odd story about the Manson murders back in the Sixties. Told to me by a longtime resident of Benedict Canyon, where the slaughter took place. It was apparently a lovely warm sunny morning. Then the milkman, who delivered to the various mansions in the canyon, was running from house to house, tears on his face. He kept saying "The blood, you've never seen such blood!" The next day everyone in Beverly Hills bought large dogs. A hush descended on the city.

People here are buying large dogs again, two at a time. Gates and doors stay locked, and telephone messages are not returned. Too much talk can be bad. And this is a town where too much of a good thing is the way it is.

I am invited to the hundredth-birthday celebration for Marion Davies, the droopy-eyed blond protégé of William Randolph Hearst and the only mistress of San Simeon. Mind you, Marion kicked the bucket many years ago, but I accept the invitation, as I am a fan, and I am curious to see who will attend.

There is a definite, rather jolly morbidity when toasting a dead movie star, and at our table vodka martinis and champagne keep coming, just the way Marion would have wanted it. Our party takes place at Arbuckle's, a restaurant on La Cienega with low ceilings, fireplaces, bad food and posters of Fatty Arbuckle and Gloria Swanson, and other silent stars, their smiling faces haunted, watching us.

I am sitting with a group of film historians and several silent movie archivists. Jane Wyatt shows up, to many whispers of "God, she still looks good," and then Charles Pierce arrives, saying "I've always loved Marion, what a gal." Girls of about sixteen sit in corners of the restaurant pretending to be Marion Davies, down to her bee-stung lips and curled blond hair. A drag queen named Alexis del Lago arrives. She is wearing a huge black fur Cossack hat and more makeup than Marla Maples Trump. Alexis waves to no one in particular and then is seated behind a column. Smart staff.

During the main part of dinner at our table we discuss unsolved Hollywood murders. I state that I feel the Black Dahlia case has been solved. A middle-aged woman, the daughter of an average Joe in Torrance, suddenly remembered in later years seeing the Black Dahlia tied up in her father's garage. She was not allowed in again. Because her father tortured the Black Dahlia for several days before neatly cutting the woman in half, draining all the blood out of the corpse and then arranging the pieces in a vacant lot off Crenshaw Boulevard. "I believe her story," I say quietly.

"Hogwash. The killer will never be named. He got away, and he's been dead a long while," says Mike, a film archivist.

"Well, what about Fatty Arbuckle? He raped Virginia Rappe during an orgy at his hotel suite in San Francisco with a Coke bottle, for God's sake. And she died of peritonitis," I countered.

"Arbuckle was acquitted twice," my new friend says. "Besides, everyone that knew Arbuckle said he was a sweet, kind man."

"Who now? Everyone's dead."

"That's not true. Buddy Rogers, Mary Pickford's husband, he's still alive. He knew Arbuckle. And Vera Burnett, over at the other table. She was Marion's stand-in from 1926 to 1936. She knew Arbuckle."

Sometimes I like to argue.

"What about William Ince? It's common knowledge Ince was screwing Marion aboard the Hearst yacht, the *Oneida,* and Hearst found them and shot Ince, then dumped his body in Santa Monica Bay. And it's also common knowledge that Louella Parsons was aboard that day and she saw everything. She held that over Hearst until the day she died, and that's why she was the queen bee of Hollywood."

I start to blush. I forgot how much I know about such things. I am slightly embarrassed.

"That's true," my new friend says begrudgingly.

An elderly woman is escorted to our table by a silver-haired man. The woman is Vera Burnett and she is ninety-six years old. She grips my hand firmly. Vera has huge blue eyes, just like Marion, and spun white hair. She is dressed in black velvet. She smiles as we speak, looking right through me.

"You look like one of Marion's old crowd," she says quite seriously to me. I don't know whether to be amused or to say thank you. I smile graciously, murmur something meaningless.

We are asked to take a formal picture, standing. Lea Sullivan, a close friend of Marion's right up to the end, is standing next to me. Vera Burnett is there, and Jane Wyatt, and others. I suddenly shiver. I know this is a picture that winds up in a book somewhere, with our names listed counterclockwise. I am still thirty-nine years old, I reason. I am still too young to be historic.

The silver-haired man smiles and asks me if I am going to the Silent Movie next to see *Peg o' My Heart* with Marion, followed by a big birthday cake with one hundred candles and Marion's face done in icing, and I say no, I'm just here for the dinner. He tells me Larry Austin would love to meet me.

We shake hands.

Marion Davies's dinner is held on January 11, a Saturday night, even though her actual birthday is January 3. One week later, a gunman enters the lobby of the Silent Movie and empties the cash register, then shoots Larry Austin through the skull. A nineteen-year-old girl who works for Austin selling popcorn and candies and cola is shot in the chest.

The theater is full. Many of the patrons are regulars, including film buffs, young directors and screenwriters. The gunman runs down the aisle, shooting randomly in the air, before disappearing through a back door. A stupid man, he is not wearing a mask. He will be identified. People at first think it's a joke, some kind of old-time Hollywood stunt, then there are screams and people duck and run for cover. A silent comedy short is being shown, leading up to the feature. It is *The Golf Adventure,* with Monty Banks. The film plays itself out and stops.

I start getting calls the next day. "Did you hear?" my friends ask. "Isn't it horrible? They killed the man who ran the Silent Movie Theater."

"What do you mean, 'they'?" I ask. My brain is beginning to dissect this tragedy. I hear varied reports. It was a junkie who killed him. It was a gang member staking territory. It was "just another" psycho. I listen to everything. Then Larry Austin is front-page news in the Sunday *Los Angeles Times*.

I discover Larry Austin was the son of William Austin, a silent film actor who starred opposite Clara Bow in the notorious film *It*. Larry Austin loved movies, and wanted to be part of them all his life. Quite coyly he refused to give his age, which was somewhere past seventy. Mature. A mature gentleman. Larry Austin believed in the complete and utter power of film.

January 23, 1997. I get a phone call this morning from an unidentified source.

"Don't use my name," the voice, definitely female, whispers into the receiver, " 'cause you know, the killer's out there. The girl at the concession stand, she saw him, she knows who he is."

"Just like Louella," I add cryptically.

"There's more. The murder was a hit. Larry Austin was being blackmailed; he was the victim of extortion by someone he knew. Larry Austin decided to stop paying and his buddy hired a hit man to kill him. Everyone knows. Everyone in town."

Prior to this phone call I listened to a radio report about Autumn Jackson, claiming to be Bill Cosby's illegitimate daughter and wanting a sincerity blackmail payment of forty-three million dollars. She phoned in her blackmail demands from a Holiday Inn in the East

San Fernando Valley. Where rooms run over one hundred dollars a night, sometimes less if you live there by the month. Then Autumn decides to accept twenty-five million. This is a loss of seventeen million dollars. Seventeen million dollars is a lot of cash to lose in a telephone conversation. Obviously this girl isn't wrapped too tight.

I think, Tread lightly, Hollywood is a small town with a killer on the loose. I value my health. I decide to zero in.

"What do you mean, buddy? Was this an ex-lover of Larry's? No one cares anymore if someone is gay," I said quickly.

"He had something on Larry Austin. Something worth a lot of money."

"Why are you calling me?"

"Everyone at the dinner was talking about you, Mr. Rawley. We know you're writing an article on Marion."

"That's true," I say. I feel a chill on my spine. I do not like the royal "we." It is coarse and frightening.

"Can I meet you for lunch?" I ask.

"No."

"We can go someplace no one goes. I know lots of places to disappear," I say brightly.

"No. Not until the police get him. It was a hit, Mr. Rawley. It was a hit and everyone knows it, but no one's talking. And you know why? Because we all know who it is."

What a hustle, I think to myself. Larry Austin's killer was one of thousands of young, talentless people who come here every day. They're looking for a divorcée, an old queen with money, an Arab with cash who'll take care of them. Their looks fade fast. They steal, sleep around. "Destroy and conquer" is an old Hollywood saying. Larry Austin was a Mormon, and the Mormon Church is currently looking for his will but cannot find it. So many secrets. We love our secrets in Hollywood. It's what makes us tick.

The picture becomes succinct. A mature gentleman is lying in a pool of blood next to the ticket booth of his theater. A frantic and terrified young screenwriter, a regular at the theater, discovers Larry and is calling 911 and the L.A.P.D. A nineteen-year-old girl struggles to walk outside, clutching her chest. Two bullet wounds. Blood is pouring down her legs.

Across town Ennis Cosby has gotten out of his car after exiting the northbound 405 freeway, which connects Beverly Hills to the Valley. It is a windy, cold night, as L.A. has had rain and storm signals of something bigger to come from the north. Ennis calls a girl on his cellular phone to come shine a light on him so he can fix his tire. This girl arrives and sees a man with a pistol. She leaves, fearing for her life. After a certain amount of time she returns to find Ennis dead, a beautiful young black man, the son of a famous entertainer, lying next to his car. She sees the man who did it, just like the girl at the Silent Movie, and suddenly the L.A.P.D. have made both women not available to the press.

Ennis's friend becomes hysterical, completely terrified, and lapses into shock. She is wearing a silver and black fox coat, very thick, rich fur, the kind of fur a whore might wear. Her blond hair is flowing in the cold night wind, and her back is to us. We will never see her face.

Somewhere in hell Louella Parsons is laughing, saying "Girls, girls, you got to get some mileage out of this. Make it work for you. I did."

Los Angeles is a camera. They are everywhere, like the paparazzi in Rome, only crueler, more conniving. Murder is perhaps one of our town's biggest selling points, not unlike Madison Avenue for New York. Murder in Hollywood is marketable.

The screen at the Silent Movie is dark. The film they would have shown that night was *Sunrise,* the first American silent by the acclaimed German director F. W. Murnau. It stars Janet Gaynor and George O'Brien. In this film Janet Gaynor is impossibly young and beautiful, and sunlight often streams through her hair, as though God has a direct interest and a good percentage of this picture.

In New York, Bill Cosby and his family emerge from their townhouse, incandescent with grief, and get into a car as photographers snap away. Ennis Cosby was a good guy. He was driving in a good part of town. The Silent Movie had a great crowd of Hollywood professionals who attended regularly.

Behind every door that leads to our dreams there lies extortion and malice. In Hollywood, flowers are poisonous, scentless, but beautiful. We put them into vases in front of picture windows where the city shimmers below us, and then go about our day, as though nothing has happened at all.

NIGHTS WITH TENNESSEE

I am often surprised by a lack of imagination. In the Nineties someone decided we cannot smoke, drink, take drugs, have sex, enjoy money and gossip. We can't dance all night, drink champagne and orange juice at dawn, wear diamonds and furs. We are not allowed to be decadent. We are not allowed laughter. We cannot fall in love and be hurt. There are just too many agendas to consider. There are just too many people who will be offended. And it stinks.

"Just wait till you're old and gray," Tennessee Williams hissed at me at six o'clock in the morning in his suite at the St. James Hotel in London. It was 1976. He was drunk and upset. I was drunk and eighteen, a student at a drama academy, and a serious habitué of nightclubs, with rich men and gorgeous young things, all ready to strike.

Tennessee was upset because I was more interested in his bodyguard, Craig Dudley, than I was in him. We had started out the evening at a discotheque called El Sombrero on Kensington High Street. Earth, Wind and Fire was big. I was dancing with Jordan from Le Sex Shoppe, and Derek Jarman.

Tennessee collapsed into my booth, smiled at me and waved. I was a tough cookie. I waved back and continued to dance. As in many nights with Tennessee, there was a bottle of red wine for him, which he drank like soda pop, and a bottle of champagne for me. I was a stickler, at the age of eighteen, for Cordon Rouge. It was either Cordon Rouge, very cold, or I didn't sit down.

Tennessee was determined to get me in bed, and I was equally determined to stay out of his. We talked and laughed. It was our fourth "date," because I didn't just go "out" with men. It had to be a date; that way they paid. Tennessee told me I had a forehead like Merle Oberon's. I thanked him and blushed. I always liked Merle.

We moved on to the next club, Maunkberry's on Jermyn Street. By this time Tennessee was on his third bottle, and he had taken two or three Seconal to relax. David Hockney walked in, looking perplexed, and then walked out. Divine was in a corner, eating six different plates of food. Sad, because Maunkberry's at that time served what I can only call "cocaine dishes": elaborate plates with tiny bits of food on them, ideal for anyone with powder in their nose and gums. I think Divine really wanted something filling. Fish and chips with vinegar and salt, rolled in a copy of the *The Times*. That would have done the trick.

The dance floor was in the back, past the overpriced restaurant. Rudolf Nureyev was dancing with a very muscular black man. Mia Farrow—and I could see tiny veins popping in her cheeks—was sitting very much alone, her hands in her lap. Elton John came in with John Reid. Rod Stewart came in with a blonde with an American accent.

It was two o'clock, and Tennessee and I moved on to a party at a Moroccan-style apartment in Knightsbridge. Which meant only one thing, of course. Black hashish. It was on this night I remember he laid his head on my lap and told me he loved me. Being a tough cookie in London in 1976, I answered quite simply, "Good for you."

At dawn we were at the St. James Hotel. Tennessee pretended to be drunk, and he always walked a straight line even when he was so loaded he could barely breathe. The doorman winked and said, "Of course, Mr. Williams, of course your friend can help you up to your suite."

Craig Dudley was asleep in the room next door. I visited Craig for what seemed to be a relatively short time, due to his ability to seize the moment, and then went back in and sat down with Tennessee, who was lying in bed in a satin robe with, of all things, a cravat in dark green and yellow paisley.

"It's July. That cravat is a bit much, I think," I said. I was no longer stoned, just drunk. At that point my alcohol and drug intake veered up and down, one of the lovely things about being eighteen.

"Then take it." He took it off and flung it at me.

"I'm old and rotten. You could make me happy, you know. I knew an angel once. He was an angel, beautiful, beautiful, but they took him away and they locked him up." Tennessee was going to cry. I'd seen it happen before, same story, and I wasn't going to buy it.

"I've got to get some rest, darling, how about tomorrow night?" I asked with a soothing voice.

He began to become belligerent, hissing at me, then

finished off one of my many nights with Tennessee with: "Remember what I said. Just wait till you're old and gray."

I have no problem remembering exactly what you said, Tennessee, even twenty years later, because you were someone who said things people remembered. I find now I am lucky to remember someone's name, much less their intellectual song.

Los Angeles has a way of taking the big shots from New York, the beauties from London and Paris, and turning them into just another rice cake. I remember I was driving a truck for a living when I heard a radio report that Tennessee had died, on the San Diego Freeway headed to Newport Beach, and I had to pull to the side of the road.

I decided then and there to quit and never look back. Soon I shall be thirty-eight, and yes, Tennessee, I am learning what it is like to be old and gray, suddenly an anachronism. All my friends from the Seventies and Eighties are dead, and we are stuck with the untalented, the not so beautiful, those who lack imagination.

I remember seeing you in Key West, in New York, briefly, and then never again. Sometimes I take out your cravat and show it to some drama types, twenty-one or -two, tops. They say, Who? And look at each other, exchanging sarcastic glances. And I realize they are now the tough cookies of Los Angeles, circa 1995.

ONE ROUGH CHICK

I n Southern California we manufacture our own gods and goddesses. Our bodybuilding stars are tanned, well oiled and muscular beyond belief, muscular to the point of not making sense. They exist to be worshiped. And as a warning. We have our Mount Olympus, and heaven likes its pound of flesh.

On Valentine's Day, 1995, Sally McNeil, then thirty-five, shot her husband Ray, then twenty-nine, in the living room of their Oceanside apartment with two shotgun blasts. Ray McNeil was black, a bodybuilder and a 1991 Mr. California. He had recently completed a commercial for Rold Gold Pretzels that aired on the January 29 Super Bowl and had been scheduled to compete in the South Florida Professional Invitational Bodybuilding Tournament. Sally was also a competitive bodybuilder. Both were ex-Marines.

The first shot lacerated his liver and severed his aorta. The second shot was fired into Ray's face, at point-blank range, after Sally had reloaded the gun. Also in the apartment were Sally's two children by a previous marriage—Shantina, then eleven, and John, nine. Shantina walked into the living room, saw Ray on the floor in a large pool of blood and ran outside, screaming. Because Sally had used a shotgun, blood was splattered all over the apartment.

Sally was not hysterical when she called 911 but stood in the kitchen looking out the window as she spoke on the phone. "I've just shot my husband," she said coolly. Ray was not yet dead. With most of his face gone, and clutching whatever guts he had left, he was slowly crawling—or trying to crawl—toward the front door. His voice can be heard in the background of the 911 taped call: a groan, a plea.

That is almost god-like strength. Or super-man, however it should be defined. Ray was full of drugs that night; the coroner's report states that his EPI-T (testosterone) level was unbelievably high. The EPI-T ratio for a normal man is 1.5; Ray's was *32.*

Sally McNeil, before the steroids and bodybuilding, was a very pretty woman; as Mrs. Ray McNeil, Sally had high blond, glamorous hair and she fancied black leather minis, high heels and a hard, hard body. Together, the McNeils were a volatile couple, desperate for recognition, awards, commercial endorsements. They were in Southern California and they wanted their pound of flesh. They were poised at bodybuilding stardom and they were going to rock and roll.

On April 19, 1996, Sally McNeil was sentenced to nineteen years to life in prison for second-degree murder. She had pleaded that Ray McNeil beat her, that she was an abused wife. The jury, after reviewing Sally's unbelievably violent history, didn't buy it.

A photograph of her face at the sentencing taken by Charlie Nueman of the *San Diego Union-Tribune* shows a woman with blond hair falling in messy wisps around her now almost masculine face. Sally's face had become broad and butch, and had begun to lack certain feminine qualities. This was a woman who was rubbing her head too much at night, awake, listening to the nothingness of prison. Lurching into a tear-filled grimace, Sally McNeil knew it was payback time.

I have been fascinated by this photo since it first appeared, then quickly disappeared, in the *Los Angeles Times*. O.J. Simpson was much better news. A tale of a white woman who kills her black husband, both of them craving recognition but physically stuck in a subculture (bodybuilding), is just not as big time as a black, heterosexual celebrity and football hero who kills his white wife.

O.J. was acquitted but found guilty in a civil court. His pound of flesh is that the Goldmans and Browns will hound him financially until the day he dies. And he knows it. Sally McNeil's pound of flesh is nineteen years to life.

It is an easy thing to kill. Ask any hunter. Aim your rifle, a bird falls out of the sky. Leave a worm on a hook in deep water, see what happens. Any serial killer will tell you how easy it is to get a girl, or a boy, in a car.

Murder never solves anything, it only ends; and with that ending comes a silence that lasts for less than a minute. A recognition for the killer. An intimacy with their victim, like a sweet perfume.

When I was six years old, I spent a summer at

camp, at the Army and Navy Academy in Carlsbad, California, above Oceanside. We swam, made burnt boxes in woodshop and lined up, little cadets that we were, for roll call, disciplines and marches. We learned how to say "Yes Sir" and "No Sir." I learned what naked men looked like.

My family had sent me there to dislodge my effeminacy, and I was a very soft, lonely and confused little boy. One day at archery, a boy named Russell was teasing me ruthlessly, calling me "girlie," and I turned, without thinking, aimed my bow and arrow and shot at him.

I was lousy at archery; the arrow whizzed by Russell and landed in a distant field, in whispering, high grass. I remember seeing a flock of seagulls scatter at the arrow, and Russell, who turned to look at me, was terrified. He began to cry.

Suddenly our instructor, an ex-Marine in his early sixties with a crew cut and gin blossoms, was in my face.

"You little faggot murderer. You sick, queer shit," he said. He then punched me in my face, so hard I fell down and passed out. I woke up in the infirmary and I was "off limits." Boys suddenly looked at me differently. I was almost a "killer." I was hot stuff.

Since then I cannot bear to be close to a weapon; even kitchen knives are difficult for me. I won't go near them. I mention this because during the writing of this article on Sally McNeil, this memory came back to me. I realized how certain things come real easy when you've been taught to kill. It's easy to shoot a bow and arrow, punch a little boy in the face, or aim a rifle at your husband. Welcome to the world of Sally McNeil.

Oceanside is one of those beach towns where success has never taken hold. The coast is lovely and flat, with a rough surf and, at certain times of the year, a kelp problem. This is not Malibu Colony living. Oceanside is gritty and gray, with a surprising lack of trees. Like Imperial Beach, Calexico, and even Yuma, Oceanside serves as a last chance. And it is one of the only beach towns in Southern California that isn't widely marketed as a resort.

This little Hades by the sea is only a matter of miles from Camp Pendleton. For over forty years, Oceanside has been the town where Marines go to get laid. But Oceanside has trailer parks, motels, bars, strip clubs, RVs, public restrooms in ratty parks, shacks and abandoned real estate, all ready for a Marine to disappear in. Oceanside has a drug culture that rivals that of Venice Beach, and it also plays host to many retired homosexuals who like it rough with a cadet from Kansas, and who know about "the trains," where sexual happenings take place, generally all male, in discarded or unlatched train cars on unused tracks.

Sally and Ray McNeil both desperately wanted out of Oceanside. They wanted to move to Venice, to be able to train at Gold's Gym on a regular basis and be part of "the scene." For the uninitiated, Gold's Gym in Venice has more muscle per square inch than anywhere on earth. This is where the stars built themselves up: Schwarzenegger, Van Damme. The Mr.

Olympias, the Mr. Californias. And it has its share of insane, aggressive bodybuilders. As I was told recently, "You need a hit man? Try Gold's Gym."

At Gold's Gym every kind of man, and woman, shows up each day to work out. Some are huge, godlike, with perfect nipples and veins running up pumped and injected arms. Some are there to stare and secretly salivate, and this sexual tension is palpable. There is a definite homoerotic air here, a worship of the greatest shrine of all, the male body. Certain women who work out at Gold's have magnificent bodies; many who compete tend toward overdevelopment. In the men's locker room men are not shy. Certainly Ray McNeil was the least shy of them all.

Sally and Ray simply couldn't afford Los Angeles, and that's why they stayed in their motel-like apartment, with one window and door, facing their parked cars. No charm here. No view. No shrubbery. No architectural details. It's the kind of apartment for people on their way down. It was just about the only way Sally could afford to keep Ray in training and feed the children and herself as well.

There is another way. Pornography and prostitution. Many male bodybuilders who consider themselves "straight" will let a homosexual photograph them for a hundred dollars. A blowjob is considerably more, and of course body worship for an hour or so can be pretty pricey. Bodybuilding is a twelve- to fourteen-hour-a-day job; income has to be supplemented.

Sally became a video "wrestler." Her professional name was "Killer" Sally McNeil, and she made a series of videos, for sale by mail order, of her wrestling men and other women. These videos are incredibly lucrative. These are not in the nude; generally a pair of shorts and brassiere, and shorts on the man, will suffice. The names of the production companies include Mass Muscle, Bare Strength Productions, Amazon Productions, Physical Culture; their products include such best-selling titles as *Women's Support Group, Muscle Tussle, Silk Stockings* and *Break In*.

There were two up and coming stars of wrestling videos. One was Lethal Legs Lee, the other was Killer Sally McNeil. Sally would also take on private wrestling matches: two hundred dollars for a half hour; three hundred for an hour. It was still not enough money to get them to Mecca.

Killer" Sally McNeil was one rough chick. A "chick" in the Nineties approximates what a "broad" was in the Forties. A "chick" is not a girl, a lady, a woman, or anything possessed of subtlety or charm. A "chick," however, is definitely female.

Recently, while driving to Palm Springs, my friend John and I argued exactly what a "chick" encompassed. Passing us at about eighty-five miles an hour, in a black Mercedes convertible, brand new, with rental tags and the top down, was this creature in her late twenties with mountains of blond hair flying around her like fire. "Discotheque," by U-2, was blaring on the radio. She wore a tiny T-shirt showing breast implants, no bra, Versace sunglasses, and had a cigarette in her mouth. Ashes flew around her, in her hair and the back of her car. She was oblivious.

"That," I said to John, "is a chick."

"I never hit Ray. I was too afraid of him."
—SALLY MCNEIL IN PRISON,
SPEAKING TO TEAGAN CLIVE

Not true. Both Sally and Ray were batterers. Women who go into competitive bodybuilding often have boyfriends or husbands who are competitive body-builders. It looks better too if a bodybuilding "couple" are also man and wife. Contests are still rated "G" and they attempt a family-oriented sensibility, but under-neath all this muscular cheerfulness is an enormous homoerotic charge.

Quite often those bodybuilding husbands and boyfriends try to control their women, and many are abusive. As I was told by a competitive female body-builder, "My husband used to beat me good if I didn't work out. But look at me. Look at me now."

Sally says she never hit Ray, but she punched an-other Marine's wife in the face because her dog bit Sally's child. Sally also beat her fourteen-year-old babysitter with a stick because she said the girl was trying to steal her husband and the girl was coming after her with two knives.

After a dispute with her ex-husband, Tony Lowdon, in 1990 over their children, Sally went ballistic, hitting Lowdon in the face, ripping off his necklace, smashing the rear and side windows of his car with an iron bar, then waving a handgun.

After the fight with her babysitter in 1986, Sally was admitted by the Marine Corps to a psychiatric ward for five days and diagnosed as a "borderline" personality. Borderline Personality Disorder is difficult to treat and counsel, as this rage, this sudden violence, is hidden under layers of abuse. Childhood trauma can be part of it. Childhood trauma could have been passed on to her daughter, Shantina, who witnessed the murder scene just minutes after it happened. Ray was still alive, almost coherent. Sally had a shotgun in her hands, and Shantina began to scream, in absolute fear and terror.

Shantina, when she was seven years old, called 911 seven years ago, at midnight, to say that Sally had left her little brother, John, and her alone. When the police attempted to handcuff Sally, she attacked them. They had to use Mace and physical force before she was subdued.

Later, in 1993, while celebrating her exit from the Marine Corps, Sally was good and drunk, dancing on a table at a bar in Allentown. Her sister was with her. During the brawl that ensued, Sally kicked and fought like a tigress. It took three policemen to subdue her: One policeman was 6'5" and 260 pounds, another 6'4" and 240 pounds, and the third cop was 5'9" and 220 pounds. Sally did not like being told to get down off the table. She kicked a bouncer in the face three times with her high heel, which broke teeth, saying over and over "I'm going to kick their fuckin' asses." She was later charged with felony aggravated assault and convicted. During this time, and sentencing, and the second-degree murder of her husband, Sally made bail and was busy making wrestling videos.

Sally took care of Ray and paid the bills. She wanted them both to become stars. She wanted money and lots of it, but by Christmas of 1994 their union was wearing thin. Sally told Ray he'd have to compete in a pro show or get a job. Then Sally found out Ray was seeing another woman and would leave her, and probably not care. Out came the shotgun.

Feeding Ray McNeil was, according to Sally, like feeding a lion. Ray McNeil could go through $170.00 worth of groceries in three days. It took a lot to keep him up.

Think six to ten chicken breasts, fried, for dinner, with cottage cheese and pineapple, steamed vegetables, nutrition drinks, vitamins, dessert. Think of a large steak, larger than anything you have eaten in a long time, then realize Ray would have three to five, rare. For lunch.

There were arguments, weights thrown out of windows, car wrecks, police interventions, and during this entire sewer of a marriage they both continued to work out.

Sally McNeil will always say she was a Marine, first and foremost. A U.S. Marine has to cover all bases, all the time. He has to have air around him. Try sitting next to a Marine, male or female, who's been in combat. You don't sit too close, or whisper in their ear, or make physical movements that aren't easy to decipher. Get too close, step over the borderline, you'll get hit. It's a reflex.

Sally had met Ray McNeil when they were both stationed at Camp Pendleton. To get Ray's ring, Sally gave up her third child, a nine-month-old boy, for adoption and divorced her husband. Fame had come calling.

Ray McNeil and Sally both took steroids. Lots of them. Thousands upon thousands of dollars worth. It is said that testosterone—great for women going through menopause, men with HIV and seniors—can often lead to aggressive behavior after continued use. But the effects of testosterone are nowhere near the results of prolonged use of anabolic steroids.

Bodybuilders will do "cocktails" of steroids, just like people with HIV do protease inhibitors. These cocktails, often called steroid "stacks," are injected and can consist of Winstrol-V, Deca-Durabolin (which made Ray McNeil bald after too much use) and Sustanon. Add Creatine Fuel, DHEA, megavitamins, protein supplements and painkillers like Nubain, a morphine derivative, on top of that. Add methamphetamine for energy. Sometimes bodybuilders will take angel dust because of its painkilling qualities but also because of the feeling of unlimited strength.

"You can lift a car. You're the strongest person alive, or at least you think you are," a bodybuilder, famous in the Eighties and now retired, pointed out to me.

"It still has not been proven completely that abuse of anabolic steroids leads to increased aggression," notes Jim Schmaltz, who edits the "Drug World" column for *Flex Magazine*.

This would explain how, during Sally's trial, prosecutor Dan Goldstein was able to get the "roid rage" part of Sally's defense thrown out almost immediately. For someone already considered "borderline," Sally's intake of steroids could very well have had her in whole new worlds, and not ones based on reality.

"If you're willing to take these drugs, it comes down to your personality," says Schmaltz. "Some can handle it. Some can't."

"I like them," I say almost deliberately. "I tried Deca-Durabolin once. My energy level was *insane*." I wait for a reply.

"You only did it once, and you're neither a competitive bodybuilder or in serious professional training. And remember, when you put on thirty, forty pounds of solid muscle, you're going to be more aggressive."

Ray McNeil was a well-liked man, and extremely handsome, terrifyingly handsome. He had big, gorgeous, soft eyes and, according to Sally, enormous genitals, and he liked to cat around. He'd had the same conservative, militaristic young adulthood as Sally, but his talent was doubtful. You don't have to be talented to be a bodybuilder; you just have to go every day and work out. Ray wanted to cross over and had tried standup comedy at a local Oceanside club.

There is a photograph after Ray had just won Mr.

California. Sally is dressed in a black leather miniskirt and patent-leather black high heels. She is smiling at Ray. She is completely, utterly in love, her Norwegian hands resting on Ray's muscle-bound, massive, sweating, dark-skinned chest. This was a man beyond sexual limits. This was a man who could make a chick go crazy.

There are also confirmed rumors that Ray and Sally performed in more than one adult film. These films are in the hands of private collectors and are not readily available. Because of Ray's endowment, a second career was considered, laughingly, in the porno business. Again, where would that leave Sally?

It has been reported that when charges were read in front of Sally before the final verdict, her face became transcendent, even euphoric, when "not guilty" was read, attached to the words "first-degree murder."

The grimace and shock that fascinated me in that photograph over a year ago was her reaction at being convicted of second-degree murder.

Perhaps, Sally thought, if I don't get first degree, they certainly won't give me second degree. What god looming above Sally still wanted its muscle and pound of flesh?

Consider this: Had Sally been convicted of first-degree murder, there could have been a book deal, film rights and considerably more media attention than two minutes on *Hard Copy* with a brief follow-up.

In a strange justification, she would have shown

Ray that one of them had actually made it; somehow, there would be success. Had "Killer" Sally McNeil been convicted of first-degree murder, she would have entered an elite Southern California group, and she would have been a star; her timing was off. Sally McNeil just wasn't a very good planner.

Her children now live with their grandparents in Pennsylvania. Sally has already been moved from one lockup to another for disciplinary problems—i.e., starting altercations with other female inmates. Complaints have been made that "Killer" Sally McNeil sings the Marine fight song at full blast when she's in the shower. *That* I would like to hear.

Sally is no fool, however. She is considering writing a screenplay (of course) about the murder and the trial, and she is currently represented by one of her wrestling video producers. One doubts this is a man who'll be sitting on the board of directors of CAA anytime soon. Sally also has her own personal Web site, where she offers poetry about love and the unknown, eagles and flying free forever, for those who want to tune in.

Teagan Clive, the only woman who has ever interviewed Sally, comes over for soft drinks and we talk. Teagan is a beautiful, tall woman, with blond, soft hair and long limbs. She is also astonishingly sharp; an incredible investigative journalist, Teagan spent fourteen months investigating Ray and Sally's life.

"You've got to understand, Donald, among athletes,

murder is not unusual. The percentage of violent crime is much higher."

We watch a video of "Killer" Sally McNeil, who introduces herself sweetly. She is incredibly muscular, wearing a cheetah-skin print thong. She has baby oil on. And a cheap, quick perm in her hair, which does not last long. She wrestles a chunky black woman named Tigra. This goes on for an hour. Halfway through, I turn and look at Teagan.

"Sally gets the strangest look in her eyes when she wrestles. She really likes to fight."

Teagan nods her head.

"Donald, Sally only knows how to fight well. She will *not submit*."

I reeled, thinking how we are all born innocent. Some of us wind up in a cheetah thong wrestling for dollars, overdeveloped and emotionally battered; and still more of us know how to aim a rifle, point a bow and arrow, or pose in an auditorium with bright lights and prizes. We forget the smell of innocence. We do what we have to. And we won't submit.

DAMAGED GOODS

"How do you find your way home in the dark?"
—MARILYN MONROE TO CLARK GABLE
AT THE END OF JOHN HUSTON'S
THE MISFITS (1961)

I forgot how powerful this scene is. Gable smiles, and for a moment we see what the greatest stars of the Twentieth Century *look like.* Utter dazzle. Faces with such impact on film I cannot look away. Gable slides his arm around the ten-Seconal-a-day Marilyn Monroe, who needed adrenaline shots laced with speed, a masseur and coffee to get her even coherent, or able to walk each morning to the set. And Gable says something like "Look to the stars, baby." He squints, points up to the clear night of a Nevada desert sky and says, "Find the biggest star in the sky, underneath it there's always a highway . . ." Camera pans away to the sky. A strange, haunting soundtrack. The most expensive black-and-white film of its day. And Arthur Miller's words, coming from a woman who would slowly lose her sanity.

Clark Gable died four days after the shooting. And of course, Marilyn died from an overdose in 1962. Then Thelma Ritter, and Montgomery Clift. Cultists call it a death film. I consider it one of John Huston's best, and most overlooked, films.

When I saw this scene I lost all my breath. I didn't see it on a video or TV adaptation, but on a 35mm screen in a producer's private home. If you don't understand Marilyn Monroe, just look at her on a big screen. Light, light everywhere, coming from her pores like she was from God.

I lost my breath because I recently read an essay by Jerry Stahl, "Inside Miss Los Angeles," in the fall 1996 issue of *Slant*. In this piece he wrote about a girl named Tammi, who had her Farrah Fawcett face; tousled blond hair, lots of makeup, who in her 8x10s looks "kind of" like Farrah Fawcett, but everything on closer inspection is "some kind of wasted landscape, a topography of scarred, pitted flesh." Now, of course, it's all faux Sharons and faux Winonas, and Jerry Stahl will pick them out every time. He points out that L.A. is "the American Haven for Damaged Goods, the town you came to so you can make enough money to leave."

I stayed. So did Jerry. We're both in our forties. I have a brunch, very elegant, with tons of flowers and French and English floral tablecloths on five tables of six. There is a buffet, under the palms and the orange trees and overlooking our pool, with steps (very Romanesque, very showgirl actually) at the deep end, winding up to an eighteenth-century, seven-foot-tall white marble statue. The effect, all things counted, is very Hollywood.

This is a writers-only brunch: all novelists, gossip columnists, screenwriters, ghostwriters, magazine editors. It will not be written about, except by me. After all, this is supposed to be our *day off*.

A flurry among the women as Jerry Stahl enters. He is a very sexy guy, completely heterosexual—and what a heterosexual he *is*, I might add. Jerry brings me flowers, orchids in a light sienna color. I thank him, lead him to the soda water, and the women, in their straw hats, teeny tiny sun dresses and high heels, encircle the poor man. Their husbands and lovers are busy pouring themselves triple vodka and cranberry juices in very tall iced tea glasses. It's going to be *that* kind of afternoon.

Jerry and I are pals. We write long letters about everything we hate, send our good writing to each other. People don't always seem to understand why a gay writer and a straight writer should get along so well, but I wave my hand. Too many labels. I am an effeminate middle-aged homosexual and my best friends are butch, actually rather dangerous, straight men. Go figure.

I tell this to Jerry when we are sitting in the shade with the *Los Angeles Magazine* nightlife editor, Nancy Rommelmann, and Jerry Stahl laughs.

"See, Donald, they just don't *get it*. We know each other."

"That we do, Jerry, that we do."

"You know where I've been, Donald."

I lower my voice, make it soft.

"Yes, I do, Jerry."

Nancy readjusts one blood-red, orange-tinged hibiscus woven through her hair and lights a cigarette. The writer Hilary Johnson, in pearl-blue sunglasses, is chatting and polishing off a bottle of white wine with Michael Woulfe, the costume designer, once under personal contract to Howard Hughes at RKO. Lots of laughter, table-hopping.

I continue: "I love the way you said Hollywood was the capital of damaged goods."

"Something like that," Jerry says, leaning in.

"You know, Donald, five years ago the doctors told me I had one year to live."

"And look at you now," Nancy pipes in with definite female admiration.

"Want to talk about needles? I know *everything* now about needles," I said brightly.

Jerry smiles.

"We'll talk about needles all you want, Donald. I'm a pro." Jerry wrote a book, for the uninitiated, about his days as a Hollywood television writer, making five grand a week and finally living out of garbage cans, a big-time junkie. The book was *Permanent Midnight.* Jerry got hepatitis C, which is slowly killing him. His liver's been shot for years, but Jerry will beat it.

What Jerry knows about me, something I've never discussed in my writing, is that I have AIDS. I've had AIDS for ten years. The past three years I almost died on more than one occasion, from spinal meningitis, kidney failure, a heart attack, pneumonia and more. And I kept going; I was determined to see my novels published, my short stories published, my essays published. Absolutely a one-track mind. Then I became one of the lucky ones. The protease inhibitor cocktails were discovered, and I was given a second chance at life, something many weren't. I treasure it. I treasure every fucking moment of my life. And Jerry knows it. He's been to the same cliff I have, and both of us on more than one occasion.

Now I'm throwing elegant poolside brunches for thirty. Six months to a year ago I was going blind from CMV, weighed 105 pounds, and had a stomach tube inserted for IV feeding. I had to walk with a walker; later

I was so weak I had to be carried by the nurse to the toilet to have my ass wiped. In a month I go to London and Brighton for a round of parties, book signings for my book of short stories. I have meetings to finalize the production of one of my short stories, "DeMarco's Jazz," into a major theatrical film. Jerry's book, *Permanent Midnight,* is being made into a film; shooting begins July 1 around Los Angeles, with Ben Stiller playing Jerry and Elizabeth Hurley as Jerry's ex-wife. I've chided Jerry Stahl about becoming "a man of myth." He pooh-poohs me. I know he's nervous, excited.

"After I come back from London, can I go on the set with you, Jerry?"

His eyes brighten.

"For lunch. Sure, that'd be fun."

My mind is already working its Hollywood trickery. Keep your sunglasses on, pick Jerry up in your 1974 perfectly restored Cadillac Fleetwood Brougham with a sunroof. I realize the air-conditioning doesn't work.

"I'll pick you up in the Caddy, Jerry. But the air-conditioning doesn't work, so we'll have to keep all the windows down and use the sunroof."

"I'll manage," Jerry says.

My Hollywood brain continues to sizzle. Maybe I'll give Elizabeth Hurley a copy of the book. She's a producer. Make a list. Figure it out.

"My car's kind of like me. Good-looking, new paint, but something's always breaking down," I say.

"Damaged goods?" Nancy asks sweetly.

Jerry and I look at her at the same time and begin to laugh.

Jerry has to leave, and I walk him to the front gate, a

white wrought-iron confection smothered in magenta bougainvillea. We shake hands.

"See you soon, kiddo," Jerry says, and he steps into the light beyond the garden.

"In July, darling. On the set." I watch him get into his car, and I think, Only a few of us are strong enough to survive the complete and utter obliteration of our souls, which get quartered, boiled and eaten by the wrong people. We build them slowly back. Our souls can't be taken away.

In this city of damaged goods, I hope to go to the set with Jerry, and after all the bullshit is done, when I'm taking him back to his apartment and his soon-to-be teenage daughter, I want to turn and look at this man and say "Jerry, how do you find your way home in the dark?"

He won't have to answer me.

DREAM CITIZEN:
1999

In the silent film *The Wind* (1927), Lillian Gish never stops sweeping up dust. To the crescendo of a symphony score, she brushes dust off her clothes, finds dust in her hair, on the food. The men are brutes in this film's distinctly nightmarish Western town; they are ugly and covered in dust. Lillian, by cue, takes one of the most astonishing faces in film and watches her window with terrified eyes. Wind is covering it with dust. It looks like an ant farm.

Today, in Los Angeles, I have a problem with dust. I can never stop sweeping out things that terrify me, and in this capital of dust they are blown in every day, by a cinema wind, under my door. Like Lillian, I clutch a certain sense of the virginal, of the still unattached soul, and I keep my eyes on the window, the ceiling; anyplace light makes itself known.

I live in a house surrounded by white walls and gardens. I know that when I step outside my world something bad will happen. When I first came to Los Angeles, in 1977, everyone was happy. Everyone was somehow blond, *somehow* connected to the film business, if even by just knowing someone. The prospects of our Southern California Hollywood lives were simple: become rich and famous.

If you can't become famous, then you can try to become rich. If you can't become rich on your own, then you marry into it. You have a house with a swimming pool. You have a maid, an Italian or German sports car, lovers, a drug habit. But you are part of the dream, of what is expected. No matter what it takes, you get there.

If you can't, then you leave. You don't stick around. This explanation is precisely the fundamental crawl that keeps Los Angeles and the last of its Hollywood dream citizens alive. I am a Hollywood dream citizen. I bought into the dream in the late Sixties, at the end of my childhood—or, I should say, I traded in one childhood for another.

This veneer of dry palms and the dust of burned scripts called Hollywood is really no more than a set of rules, a dream state. And in Los Angeles, even with the constant attention demanded by studios, like a baby whining at a milkless breast, this dream state has become an archive. Of what we wanted.

Los Angeles is basically a third-world city now; a more appropriate public relations term would be "international." Twenty years ago it wasn't. Poverty wasn't seen. There was no grime. Paint was fresh, hedges clipped. The sprinklers came on every afternoon. Now poverty is taken for granted.

At a recent luncheon at the Beverly Glen Center, at the top of Bel Air, a woman pointed out to me that "the beggars in Beverly Hills have the *gall* to ask for five dollars. A five-dollar bill! If you don't give them a five, they follow you down the street until you give them a dollar bill. And if you try to give them a quarter, or fifty cents, they throw it in the street and spit at you! That's why I do my shopping here now. They have *security guards.*"

I realized, during the course of this luncheon, that the group at our table could be anywhere in the world: dressed in saris and sunglasses and complaining about beggars at one of the better cafés in Calcutta; geography is no longer an inclusive privilege. And twenty years ago in Los Angeles, complaining about beggars would not have been an option.

I also noticed the dream was still active at this particular table. The sunglasses stayed on while we ate. Names like Sharon Stone and Julia Phillips and Barry Diller became Sharon, Julia and Diller. A toss of the hand. Who's sleeping with who. Who's broke. Who's on a rebound. Who just bought Eddie Murphy's old place on Benedict? Which was built by Cher, but who can remember?

To be honest, I enjoyed my lunch. I enjoyed the company. I like the Hollywood bullshit. It never changes. But the real community that forms Hollywood, that seizes and capsizes our desires with the regularity of an angry whale, is growing smaller, more afraid, a little dull, a little average.

I also find it continually astonishing that we take an actor's opinion at face value, and that film stars today are possessed by the kind of intellectual stamina to make important comments that the public will believe as law.

In a recent insert in *Entertainment Weekly,* Bruce Willis, pouting that Demi Moore's production of *The Scarlet Letter* was a flop with lousy reviews, went on record as saying "Is there some kind of literature cop out there who says you can't change an ending?"

With the classics, Bruce, yes, there are literature cops.

Turns out Demi's public were the cops this time. Also, after reacting to this moronic remark, it is doubtful I shall take any remark by Bruce Willis seriously again, but the rest of America will.

Yet I like Bruce and Demi. They too are Hollywood dream citizens. They have their chain of Planet Hollywood restaurants, tons of money, healthy children, a stable marriage, a gorgeous house in the hills, and an extremely large staff that adores them. The dream works on all levels here.

It is very doubtful they will have to struggle with trying to order a cheeseburger in Vietnamese, or be the object of reverse racism at a cocktail party, or be told quite sincerely by a journalist that all white people will have left Los Angeles, and Hollywood, by the year 2010. That their time is up.

I believe in black and white, light and shadow, in Panavision and Technicolor, perhaps the fact that what I see on screen is part of me, the way I speak and act. This dust blowing outside my door has no magic anymore; it's filling up the windows, getting on my clothes and in my hair, and I want to ask Lillian Gish, "How do you get rid of this dust?"

How can I become clean again, a byproduct of film, a Hollywood dream citizen? Although I am old enough, and battered enough, to know one thing. I am a citizen of an invisible city that's almost gone, and whatever will be left will be points of speculation for those who unearth it. Like Nefertiti's Armana, lying under a mile of sand.

Chasing the Shadows

The romantic in me comes out occasionally. I wish for glamour again. Tall tales, legends, black-and-white film and Josef von Sternberg's lighting of Marlene Dietrich's face. Or the way Elizabeth Taylor kissed Montgomery Clift in *A Place in the Sun.*

I am thirty-eight years old, and most people in their early twenties do not even know what I am talking about. Part of our generation is displaced. We don't know how to react to the new, hard, cold edges.

On Belfast Drive, in the expensive part of Sunset Plaza Drive in the Hollywood Hills, I am sitting in a chic house overlooking a pool and view of Los Angeles. Judging the overstuffed furniture with ivory silk upholstery, and the complete absence of books or art anywhere, I know it was decorated by a Hollywood designer. The house is warm as a coffin. I am sitting with Barry Miller, who starred in *Saturday Night Fever* with John Travolta, *The Chosen, Fame,* and one of the great flops of recent years, a film by Danny Aiello called *The Pickle.* Barry is my age. He looks ten years younger than me.

Miller has not had a good time of it in the Nineties. His eyes are shadowed. He fidgets nervously, sips mineral water quietly.

"I've had it," Barry says. "It's over for me here." He looks out over the city. "I've pissed off a lot of people. I didn't play according to the rules."

"No one tells you the rules here," I interject.

"*Hello,* I won a Tony Award for *Biloxi Blues.* For twenty years, the sadomasochism of Hollywood is they won't turn me into a has-been, but they won't make me a *star*-star either. See, people who hired me always thought they were getting the last role I ever played. But you *can't* be put into a category. Or bought and sold."

"I know a lot of people who have been bought and sold," I say cryptically.

"Hollywood is one groaning mortgage," Barry continues. "Everybody is waiting for the next thing to happen. The next money. I'm tired of chasing the shadows. I'm tired of the 'sanding away' of my aesthetics. Look, I'm self-taught. I'll go to New York, maybe Cambridge. I like Cambridge."

"You'll really leave?" My voice seems incredulous.

"Yes. I'm leaving in two days. This is my mother's house. She's never here. No one's ever *here.*" Barry gets up and opens the French doors leading out to the terrace. A blast of hot wind permeates the room.

I want to say, Well, maybe you will become just an actor, not a star, and you will work for the rest of your life. Perhaps even steadier. Isn't that good enough? Then I remember that Barry Miller has played with the big boys. Barry Miller has won awards, has had his name above the title. He's fought for years.

Barry Miller squints into the high yellow afternoon. Mexican gardeners are using leaf-blowers, and I hear the faint music of Ella Fitzgerald coming from a house down the hill.

"It's like a snake biting its own tail," Barry whispers sadly. "And someday there'll be nothing left."

DON'T
DARLING ME

Today, in late May, Jane Greer sits down with me in her Bel Air living room. Looking at her, I think, Some of us *do* survive. We age graciously, we continue on with life. We stay in Hollywood.

There is a sense that Hollywood time is not important to Jane Greer, that perhaps it never was. She has two African gray parrots who are always fighting, among other birds and animals that have the run of her rambling home. The African grays eye each other and pace back and forth. One parrot echoes "Darling! Darling!" while the other mutters "Don't darling me! Don't darling me!" It is the first time in a week I have laughed.

Jane Greer is a film star of the Forties and Fifties. Recently film historians have lauded many of her films at RKO as film noir masterpieces, like *Out of the Past,* with Robert Mitchum. In the Eighties, director Taylor Hackford made a remake of *Out of the Past,* called *Against All Odds*, and Jane Greer had a supporting role.

"I was brought to Hollywood by Howard Hughes in 1943. That was my first studio contract," Greer says, a softness coming into her voice.

"He was nuts," I confer.

"I knew Howard pretty well. And, yes, I'd have to say

you're right." Greer laughs, an elegant, kind laugh. Her hair is white now.

"My favorite story about Hughes," I continue, "is when he bought RKO. He never set foot on the lot. Except to purchase it; he drove to RKO at night in a limousine with shaded windows. Top secret. When he bought the studio the next day, he was asked what he wanted done, and he said—"

"Paint it!" Greer cuts in, laughing. "You know, I was lucky. I loved the studio system. Sometimes on days off, I'd still go on the lot, just to have lunch at the commissary and breathe it in. I never got tired of it. Never."

"Stars today have to be their own corporation. Their image has to be commercial enough for them to get roles and buy films that will show their talent," I say. Greer nods her head.

"See, in the studio says, that was taken care of. They built me from small parts to starring roles over a period of years. They groomed me. Developed an image that worked."

Greer pauses. Her living room is subdued and cozy. I remind myself there is a family that has grown up here.

"I was watching *Out of the Past* several nights ago on one of those classic movie channels," Greer confides, "and I started thinking how Jacques Tourneur, the director, was so brilliant. He said to me, 'Jane, in this film, no big eyes. First half of film: good girl. Second half of film: bad girl.'"

"That's easy directions."

"I only wish the glamour was the same. But things change. Two friends of mine, Joan Crawford and Joan

Bennett, were the most glamorous women in Hollywood. They were unbelievably gorgeous. Unreal. And neither would leave their front door unless they were *dressed*."

"Sharon Stone is like that today. She's always presenting the image of a star."

"True. Oh, if you could have known what a Hollywood studio was like! One day, at the RKO commissary, I was having lunch with costumed extras: fourteen pirates and four Abraham Lincolns at one table!"

"I can imagine," I say dryly.

"I was filming *Sinbad the Sailor* with Maureen O'Hara. Douglas Fairbanks, Jr. Cary Grant was making a picture on the lot. It seemed everyone was working then. Every soundstage was full, you know?"

"Of course."

"I had invited a high-school friend to lunch at the RKO commissary. I met him at the gate, gave him a pass, and we had lunch. At the table I whispered to him, 'Do you know who you're sitting next to? Maureen O'Hara and Cary Grant!' And he looked at me and said, 'Who?' He had no idea."

Jane pauses, smiling ruefully.

"I was furious. I made excuses about work, escorted him to the gate and took his pass. A lot of children used to hang out at the front gate, waiting for a glimpse of a movie star. I walked over to a boy, just a young kid, handed *him* the pass and took him for lunch with Cary Grant. It was a *wonderful* day."

I know I will sleep tonight, perhaps even dream. In my dreams I will be eating breakfast at the Peninsula Hotel, dinner at Eclipse, and everyone will know my name, point to me. I will be lit like Tyrone Power and I will never leave.

The author of *Hollywood Babylon,* Kenneth Anger, remarked once that the movies "disappoint in that they promise immortality, but don't really deliver; they get folded, spindled, and mutilated, and grow scratches like wrinkles. Their blooming colors fade, as people do. And like lovers, and people in general, they can explode in flames and disappear without a trace."

At the end of this century, movies are the promise of immortality, with new methods of preservation. Like a devil's promise, we think they will make us safe. Sitting by my pool, in the shade of a fat palm tree and an overhang of yellow bougainvillea, I am talking on a cordless phone to see what will happen next. I am scanning the morning paper, to see what will happen next. I am finishing a letter to my agent about a film deal. To see what will happen next. And when I touch my face, I can feel a new wrinkle, and before I start dialing again, I suddenly wonder when it will all explode in flames, and disappear, without a trace.

EPILOGUE

One of the hardest parts of writing on Hollywood is that you always risk the taint of cliché, and you will almost always be dated, and fast. My agent, Noah Lukeman, and I decided an epilogue was necessary, a sort of "settling of business," but nothing here in Hollywood ever settles. Quite often this town's history repeats itself in countless, amazingly dull forms, but it always moves ahead.

Each of these essays works as a set piece: a distinct, personal archive of a decade spent in a city I have lived *way* too long in. I believe, for a writer, certain memory and thought should attempt posterity; whether or not they make it as history is strictly dice on felt.

The only essay I decided to postdate is "Dream Citizen: 1999," as it just seemed the right thing to do. The dream is still alive in me and certainly won't end in 1999, but what a last year to what a century! After 2000, everything is going to change in countless, unseen ways.

Perhaps a hundred years from now, Hollywood will be a curiosity, like a Ford Model-T. Perhaps, as The Who showed in their rock opera *Tommy*, there will be a church of Marilyn Monroe and we will all be gods in a new, celluloid mythology. Perhaps a hundred years from now, those of us who lived and made and chronicled Hollywood will look like complete idiots. *That* is a distinct possibility.

I have always considered the use of the word *fuck* the mark of an amateur writer, but I have to admit, we are a fucking weird bunch here by the Pacific. In a July 1, 1997, article in the *New York Times,* it was reported that Todd Michael Volpe, who advised Hollywood celebrities on building their art collections, actually defrauded them to the tune of $2.5 million. Art deals gone bad. Money not returned. Fake art. Sounds like a movie.

Of course Volpe would be caught, but his client list was impressive. Volpe, 48, had Jack Nicholson as a business partner for art investments—except Nicholson never saw a quarter, or a nickel. Joel Silver, Nicholson, Barbra Streisand and my favorite dartboard, Bruce Willis, were clients. Kathleen Kennedy and Frank Marshall, famous producers, were taken to the cleaners for about $83,000.00.

That is not a whole lot of money in Hollywood; Volpe—again, like so many of us—was dealing in Hollywood time and Hollywood money, but he was smart enough to understand the sheer sexual value of cash in hand.

"What happened was that he [Volpe] moved to California and got into the California lifestyle, which was above his means, and you rob Peter to pay Paul. And all of a sudden it fell apart on him," stated Robert Colbert, Nicholson's business manager.

That's a very kind attitude, if you ask me. But Mr. Colbert, if he is a good business manager, has arranged this as a loss on Mr. Nicholson's tax returns. Nicholson, who is worth millions, will make more movies. People will forget, here.

The power structure has remained intact, albeit changed in small ways. But Mark Canton, my least favorite studio head, was let go at Sony with a lip-licking relish. Canton lost me when he piped up in the press about moviemaking "being like baseball, we're all team players!" or some such dull-witted bon mot, and after that I watched Sony lose *millions*. That gosh oh gee attitude is fine and dandy for the head of a scout troop, but not the head of a studio.

Dreamworks, the studio started by Spielberg, Geffen and Katzenberg, is moving into the millennium with great tenacity and aplomb. It wants to build its studio on semi-marshland between Playa and Marina del Rey. Environmentalists are up in arms, but in all honesty there aren't too many rare whooping cranes in this area, and a little voice tells me the studio will be built.

I hear from many fellow writers of a general confusion among the lesser executives at Dreamworks that bodes well, in my opinion. Seems like no one is quite sure what decisions they are allowed to make. Sounds like a studio to me. It's the oldest Hollywood trick in the book, and it drives writers *insane*.

Andrea, the twenty-nine-year-old wife of a production head, has divorced her husband and moved to a very grand Charlottesville, Virginia, estate, with a woman.

My screaming producer, Michael, is still screaming. He hasn't had a good picture in five years.

In writing about Hollywood I tried to explain, quite clearly, the mechanics of a clock. Self-winding, this clock never breaks down and tells perfect time, but you've got to keep it in good shape. You have to keep winding it up in Hollywood, or your ticker won't start. What you expect from Hollywood, you get.

"Little Ghosts" was written because something, or someone, told me not to let the deaths of these children just disappear. There is still an oppressively high rate of child and infant abuse in Los Angeles's last suburb. In Palmdale they are still coping by extending therapy programs; that is, if a young couple are willing to admit they have a problem.

The real danger, hooded and fanged, was, and still is, methamphetamine. At the time of my writing, meth labs were expensive. Home labs, like the ones I saw in trailers, were cheap but dangerous. That has changed. People have gotten considerably more sophisticated. As with any poison, we want more and more of it.

According to an article in the *New York Times,* the Midwest has taken up home methamphetamine manufacture with a vengeance. From Blue Springs, Montana, to small dust-bowl towns in Kansas, this kind of speed has become the small-town Midwesterner's drug of choice.

This is utterly terrifying. I have stated publicly on radio programs that I consider methamphetamine the new murder drug. And it is. Take enough of it and you will destroy your looks and health. Take even more and you will wind up killing someone. That's the way it is. Michael P. Shanahan, a retired agent of the Federal Bureau of Investigation, adds: "It's American ingenuity at its worst."

I have always been a nervous man; that is what possibly made me such a terrifically sincere alcoholic. My nerves were numb. For ten years. During the writing of "Little Ghosts," I couldn't put in some of the worst atrocities done to children, like the body of a baby girl found in a small plastic trashcan filled with quick-drying cement. These are *commonplace.* Emotionally and spiritually I broke down, closing my doors, after I finished "Little Ghosts," and it took me quite a while to recover.

Most certainly Tippi Hedren has more big cats. She is always a rescuer, a hard job indeed. At the time I wrote "Our Lady of the Lions" we were all set to publish in *Buzz,* everyone loved it, then things became delayed and finally canceled. This is not unusual in the magazine business. One editor finally spilled the beans. The article wasn't sexy enough. I replied, Tigers aren't sexy? Movie stars aren't sexy? To which I was told, "Movie stars and tigers are sexy when they are under thirty and have a hundred mil gross on their latest picture. Then they're sexy." A quick, succinct lesson in publishing.

In the last several years Hedren has hosted several Shambala fundraisers, with everyone in the Hollywood alphabet attending, quite successfully. At the premiere of *Evita* I saw her sitting at one of the front tables, near the tango band, with her grandchildren. Melanie and Antonio were a few yards away, smothered in photographers and the white light of flash cubes. Tippi had a big, simple smile on her face. She looked like a very content lioness. I did not go over and say hello. It would have wrecked the moment for both of us.

A murder suspect has been found in the slaying of Ennis Cosby, and Autumn Jackson, the so-called "daughter" of Bill Cosby, is looking at twenty-six months in prison. Quite a price to pay for fifteen minutes of fame.

Bill Cosby has had to admit publicly, which he has done with simplicity and grace, the details of a minor, really rather shitty, extramarital affair with Autumn's mother. Bill is a heterosexual, sexually active, healthy black American male. We should finally start being honest with ourselves and admit that most men will have the odd affair. French women understand this. Life goes on.

Larry Austin's murderer has been found. His name is James Van Sickle, and he was basically both Austin's lover and the projectionist at the Silent Movie. Samantha Dunn told me of Larry Austin's funeral, the hushed whispers in the Hollywood sun, and the strange fact that he was buried specifically next to an elderly man whose marker reads "World's Greatest Movie Fan." Of course, I reasoned. Of course. This man who died in the late Eighties, and whom Larry Austin is now buried next to, was his lover. This was the man who instilled in Larry the idea of obtaining the Silent Movie and running it as his own. Movies were what they both loved. Movies and dreams.

Several mornings ago I learned Gianni Versace was murdered, execution style, by a notorious San Diego serial killer, outside his palace in Miami Beach. For the last few days every journalist in town has been scrambling to somehow tie this tragedy to Los Angeles. The results have been amusing.

Articles, quite insipid, have come out in the *Los Angeles Times* on the similarities of Miami Beach and Los

Angeles: hot weather, beautiful people, celebrities. "Wowee!" is all I can counter. And the fact that the suspect hails from *Southern California*. I honestly believe the powers that be would have preferred to see this murder happen in Bel Air, or Beverly Hills. Think of the press. Think of how quickly the film rights would be snapped up. I find it vile. And scary too.

Las Vegas has not let up one inch. People still go there to lose money, start a new life, lose more money, kill themselves. More mega-casino-hotel-resort-wonderlands have sprung up, including New York-New York and the Monte Carlo. The Rat Pack's old hangout, the Sands, a hotel I loved, as did everyone, was blown up recently. Matches from the old Sands now go for fifty dollars a book, casino chips a lot more. That's how they get things done in Las Vegas. They blow everything up.

Sally McNeil is still in prison. We are *not* corresponding.

I haven't spoken to Jane Greer recently, but I understand she's doing well. My lover John had an art show here at the house and Jane came by, looking quite regal, and stayed all afternoon. I haven't seen or spoken to Barry Miller in quite some time. He sent me a script he wrote, full of angst and bad dialogue, and I had the unpleasant business of telling him so on his service. I wish him well, though. For that brief time I spoke with him, he made me see things with exquisite clarity, and all from his point of view. Which, of course, is the mark of an exceptional actor.

Wolfgang Petersen is, I'm quite certain, ready to either start filming or has already finished a project. That's his life. He is not a man one disturbs with incidental telephone calls. "How the hell are ya" does not work here.

My very good friend James Kersey, at Harry Winston, comes by for drinks now and then and we always laugh. He calls himself "the Last Virginia WASP" in Beverly Hills. I, of course, have discovered that those wonderful folks at Winston have also put out a solid gold kaleidoscope; all the little stones inside that form patterns are rubies, sapphires, emeralds and diamonds.

When the ultimates are pinpointed in a lifetime, as I have tried to do, their status quo changes little. But here in this city of damaged goods, money, slander, joy and energy, one should always be reminded what an ultimate is. What we have created to desire, and what we abhor.

Best wishes from Hollywood.